DEALING WITH
GRIEF
AND HOW TO MOVE BEYOND IT

KEIA K. HOLT

ISBN: 979-8-9990346-0-1 Paperback

ISBN: 979-8-9990346-1-8 eBook

CONTENTS

DEDICATION

In memory of my parents, Tyree and Jackie Holt. They supported me in everything that I did in school, sports and all my other extracurricular activities. I used to read my stories for the newspaper and yearbook to them before they were printed. I never imagined that I would write a book about the grief that I experienced from their deaths. But I believe they would both be pleased with the outcome. I can imagine my father giving one head nod in approval.

Thank you to my friends and family who encouraged me along the way as I was writing this book. Thank you for confirming the need for the book and helping me to overcome my insecurity about sharing my story. Our families have suffered much grief. But we have also lived to tell the story. Thank you for sharing your grief with me and for bearing mine. I cannot begin to list all your names. You know who you are, and I love you.

I am grateful for my editor, Amy Barham. I prayed for the type of editor that I wanted, and God connected me with the perfect person. She has great insight, attention to detail and she is a woman of God. I appreciated her words of encouragement and her feedback. I wasn't sure what to expect with an editor, but this experience was so great, that I think I'll write another book.

WHY SHOULD YOU READ THIS BOOK?

Maybe you aren't experiencing grief right now, but as we all know, we will eventually lose friends and loved ones. Grief doesn't play favorites; it will visit us all. So, if you don't buy this book for yourself, then buy it for a friend or loved one.

Grief is defined as "keen mental suffering or distress over affliction or loss; sharp sorrow; painful regret."[1] Grief is usually associated with the loss of a loved one. But grief can be caused by many things including divorce, losing or changing jobs, moving, change in financial status, broken friendships, loss of faith, or the death of a pet.[2]

I'm not a grief expert, but I can say that I've experienced grief, dealt with it, and moved beyond it. My introduction to grief began at a young age with my mother's cancer diagnosis. It continued off and on for nearly a decade before she died. I was eighteen; she was thirty-five. That, more than any other loss that I have suffered, has shaped me into who I am.

My mother's illness and death were my introduction to grief, but unfortunately, that was not the final chapter.

My story includes the loss of some family members and one tragic relationship. Each loss affected me differently, and my response to grief changed over time. There were some very challenging times in my life, but by the grace of God I grew stronger in Christ and I survived. I am "Whole but Holey" (see the poem later in the book).

I have included scriptures that, as a pastor, I believe will bring comfort to those who are grieving. While we all need to learn how to deal with grief, none of us need to remain in a state of grief. I don't have an exact formula (I don't believe there is one), but I am sharing my story, and I pray that it helps someone.

The Butterfly

I asked my friend Shelby to design a book cover for me. I had a vision of an androgenous person starting out in gray and blue tones on the left of the cover and transitioning into brighter colors toward the right of the cover. I wanted to show the transition from "Dealing with Grief" to "Moving Beyond It." Over time she kept working on different ideas, but I hadn't seen any of them yet.

During one of our weekly gym sessions, Shelby told me that some of her ideas were different than what I requested. I reminded her that I'm not artistic and I was open to her ideas. She said that one of them was a butterfly. We got off the treadmill and started the weightlifting routine. My mind kept going back to the butterfly. In between sets I said, "A butterfly represents change. I like it." Well, Shelby got busy with better paying gigs, and I reached out to another designer for help. But I told Shelby, "I'm totally stealing your idea!"

Butterflies have four stages of metamorphosis: egg, larva, pupa, and adult. The difference between the stages of grief and the metamorphosis of the butterfly is that a butterfly's transition is linear, and the timing of the butterfly's change is known. Our grief is not linear. It is not timed, and it is not always the same. Grief can be different with each death. The third experience with loss may not hurt as much as the first loss. That doesn't mean that you love that person less; it's just that you're learning how to deal with grief.

If you ever look at the pictures of the butterfly in its different stages, they aren't pretty. But each stage has a purpose, and it is important for the egg, larva, and pupa to make it to the next stage. That's just like dealing with our grief. It isn't pretty, but it is purposeful. The emphasis is not about being beautiful at the end but about surviving to the end, striving for the time to spread your wings and fly. Inhale . . . Exhale . . . Breathe! You are alive! Now live!

DEFINING GRIEF

What is grief? "Grief is a reaction to loss, and like a fingerprint, it is different for everyone."[3] When we lose someone we love, we experience grief, mourning, and bereavement. These are similar terms, but they have different meanings. *Grief* is our reaction to a loss. Just like each person is unique, the way we grieve them will be unique as well. *Mourning* is how we express our grief in public. Mourning practices differ amongst various cultures, religions, and regions of the world. In the Bible, people would mourn by tearing their clothes, wearing sackcloth, and covering themselves in ashes (for examples, see Genesis 37:34; Esther 4:1; Job 2:8). *Bereavement* refers to that specific period of mourning. People often take bereavement leave from work after the death of a loved one. They set aside time to grieve and take care of the needs that arise after the loss of a loved one like funeral arrangements, finances, and to meet the needs of their family.

Funeral arrangements are not new to humanity. In Genesis 23, the whole chapter talks about Abraham's concern for his wife's burial place. We do the same thing when we fret about what to bury our loved one in, where to place the plot, or what to put on the headstone. We honor our loved one until the very end, just like they did in the Bible. Funerals in the Old Testament were similar to today. When a loved one died, the whole family or tribe would gather. When prominent people died, the nation grieved together. For example, when Moses died, the people mourned together for thirty days (Deuteronomy 34:8).

There were professional mourners during biblical times. Jeremiah 9:17–18 says, "This is what the LORD of Heaven's Armies says: 'Consider all this, and call for the mourners. Send for the women who mourn at funerals. Quick! Begin your weeping! Let the tears flow from your eyes.'" Weeping and wailing at funerals was just as common then as it is now. One of the shortest verses in the Bible is, "Jesus wept" (John 11:35 NIV). This was at Lazarus's burial. To mourn or to grieve is part of the process of dealing with grief.

Elisabeth Kübler-Ross introduced the five stages of grief in her book, *On Death and Dying*, which have now become widely accepted: denial, anger, bargaining, depression, and acceptance. These stages help us process loss and adapt successfully to changes in our realities. We don't all experience all five stages, nor do we process each stage the same way. Some stages last longer than others, and it's perfectly normal to revisit stages.

It is important to work your way through whichever stage you are feeling. There aren't any shortcuts to moving beyond grief, and there aren't any time limits. Some stages might be shorter than others, while others may be longer. Remember, there aren't many rules when you're dealing with grief. But do not self-medicate or do harmful things to yourself. It may feel like a relief at the time, but it's a temporary solution with permanent consequences.

Grief can be triggered by many events, not just the death of a loved one. A breakup or divorce, loss of a pet, losing a job or financial stability, pregnancy loss, or even retirement, can all be a source of grief in one's life. These are all significant losses, and it's important to recognize that. I remember decades ago one of my coworkers was crying off and on during the day. Each time I asked what was wrong, she said, "Nothing." I finally pulled her to a quiet spot in the office and asked her again. She said that her horse died. She didn't say anything to us because she didn't think we would understand. Remember that grief is personal. If the loss is important to you, then it's important, and it's appropriate to grieve that loss.

Denial is the initial period after a loss in which the grieving person does not accept the reality of the loss. It's not that they don't understand, but that it hasn't sunk in yet. I experienced denial with my mother's death. Her cancer had gone into remission two times before, so I believed that it would this time, too. Even though I saw signs that this time was different, I didn't want to believe it. Sometimes the way to deal with grief at this stage is to deny that it's happening or has happened. Some examples of denial are:

> "I don't want to talk about it; it's not real."
> "I didn't see their body, so I don't believe it."
> "He/she wasn't sick enough to die!"

As you transition out of the denial stage, you may experience new emotions that were suppressed before, like sorrow.[4] When I came home from college, my mother told me that she didn't have any scheduled doctor's appointments because they could not help her anymore. They predicted her heart would stop beating on December 26, 1990. Our family discussed DNR (do not resuscitate). Later that night I cried in my room, as I could no longer deny that my mother was going to die. Coming out of the denial stage is a blessing; it's a sign that you're healing. And you may not feel like it, but you're getting stronger emotionally. "Denial allows you time to adjust to who you are, where you are, and what your next step will be following a loss."[5]

Anger is rational and irrational at the same time. It is a rational feeling after losing a loved one, but the anger is irrational because it is often misplaced. "Where denial may be considered a coping mechanism, anger is a masking effect. Anger is hiding many of the emotions and pain you carry."[6] We may mask anger, by redirecting anger toward ourselves, our deceased loved ones, family members, doctors, or even God. This kind of anger can be unpredictable and hurtful. Some examples of anger are:

"Why didn't he/she take better care of themselves?"
"God, if you were real, you wouldn't let my loved one die!"
"God, if you loved me, you would save my loved one."
"I think the doctor did something. He/she didn't care about my loved one."

My grandmother told me to prepare myself because my mother was going to die soon. I kept telling her that she was wrong; it was just a setback. She softly told me that it wasn't. My reaction was to curse her out and tell her that she didn't know what she was talking about. I hung up on her. I sat in the phone booth and just cried. A part of me knew that she was right. But I didn't want to hear it. And I wasn't ready for my mother to die. My anger was directed at my grandmother, but it wasn't her fault that my mother was dying of cancer. My grandmother was trying to help, and I lashed out at her. This is an example of the denial and anger stages at the same time.

For those who may be comforting someone who is grieving, you may hear, "No one is helping me. No one knows what I'm going through. No one understands. No one, no one, no one!" This can be very hurtful to hear when you are the "no one" who has been helping. But we must remember that the anger stage is not the rational stage. I have often had to tell myself what I'm telling you, "Don't take it personally."

Remember that everyone may not experience all stages of grief. I remember when my father died, a coworker asked me if I had experienced the anger stage yet. I said, "No," and her response was, "You will." That wasn't accurate. I went through the anger stage with my grandmother's death, but with my father, I was hurt, and I missed him, but I was never angry about his death. So, if you don't experience all stages, or if some are short while others last longer, please know that it's OK and perfectly normal.

Bargaining is a way of coping when you feel helpless. Death is happening and we cannot do anything about it. "One of the most compelling is the bargaining stage of grief—a time during which an individual struggles to comprehend how to accept the loss of a loved one, possession, job, or something else."[7] We begin wondering what could have been done differently, wishing there was a way to change the outcome. Guilt seems to be a part of the bargaining stage. But just because we feel guilty does not mean that we are; remember, feelings aren't always rational. Some examples of bargaining are:

"I should have demanded that the doctors do more."

"Maybe if I had treated him/her better, this wouldn't have happened."

"God if you heal (or save) my loved one, I'll start (or stop) _____."

Depression can cause one to feel sad and hopeless after the loss of a loved one. During this period, you may withdraw from people and your usual schedule. You may spend more time sleeping; you may stop taking care of yourself. You may need to seek some additional help to deal with your grief, and that's OK. Remember that grief is like a fingerprint—it is unique to each person and the effects of each death on you can be different, too. Some examples of the depression stage are:

"I'm going to quit (insert activity). It won't be fun without my loved one."

"I can't live without my loved one."

"I can get through this on my own."

"I'll never be happy again."

"Bereavement can lead to prolonged grief disorder if these feelings persist and continue to cause significant impairment and distress in your life for more than a year."[8] This is a diagnosable condition. It can be difficult when you finally realize that your loved one isn't coming back, that this time is different than before, and that can be depressing.[9] Let someone know that you need help. That help can come in many forms; it doesn't have to be just one. You may connect with a friend, counselor, grief group, or find a combination of them all. Choose to live and not just exist.

Examine yourself and your life. Are you taking care of yourself? Even when you are grieving the loss of a loved one or one who is terminally ill, you still must maintain your health. Are you sleeping and eating well? Are you allowing others to comfort you during your time of grieving? Please don't isolate yourself. And please keep your health, mental and physical, a priority. You still matter. Don't lose hope! Keep working through your grief; it is possible to get through this.

Acceptance is coming to the realization that our loved one is physically gone and they are not coming back. Acceptance does not mean that we're happy our loved one is gone, but we must acknowledge and accept that they are. Now we must figure out how to live our lives without their presence while holding on to their memory.

Dr. Judy Ho says that the stages of grief are more circular than linear.[10] "For example, you may feel like you've accepted the loss, then something happens months later, and you circle back to denial. That's a very natural and realistic way of thinking—don't feel like you're taking steps back."[11] I can attest that: as I processed my mother's death, there were times that I cycled back to denial. I just couldn't believe she didn't get better this time. This is how some people deal with grief, and it is normal.

Psychologists Melinda Smith, Lawrence Robinson, and Jeanne Segal offer this helpful list of steps to dealing with grief and moving beyond it:

1. Acknowledge your pain.
2. Accept that grief can trigger many different and unexpected emotions.
3. Understand that your grieving process will be unique to you.
4. Seek out face-to-face support from people who care about you.

5. Support yourself emotionally by taking care of yourself physically.
6. Recognize the difference between grief and depression. [12]

Some examples from the acceptance stage are:

> "God, I miss my loved one, but I know that you will help me to heal."
>
> "I accept that my loved one is gone, but I know that they aren't suffering anymore. I take comfort in that."
>
> "It's OK for me to live my life. That's what they would want me to do."

Unresolved grief can affect your relationships with others. Take notice if you find yourself lashing out at others. You may not be mad at them, just upset about what you're dealing with. I believe anyone who is reading this book wants to deal with their grief and move beyond it. You have already figured out that it isn't easy. But for those of us on the other side of our grief, I believe we will all say that dealing with grief is important and worth it.

The stages of grief can be like a staircase. You're taking one step at a time. If you have to go backwards, don't worry, the other steps will still be there. But as long as you keep moving, you will reach your destination.

MY MOTHER—JACQUELINE
EVON HOLT, 1990

When I was in elementary school, I knew that my mother was sick. She had to go into the hospital. I was never told exactly why. I can't remember what my father said, but neither he nor my mother ever openly discussed it. That was the first hospitalization that I remember. She wasn't properly diagnosed with cancer for another three years. I watched her suffer with cancer in Germany, New Jersey, Alaska, and finally in Washington (my father was in the Army). The cancer would go into remission, and then a couple years later, it would come back. But God did not call her home until 1990. I was eighteen years old, and my brother, Alex, was twenty. My mother was thirty-five, and my father was thirty-seven. We were a young family. My mother's death had the biggest impact on me because she was the first death that I experienced, her illness lasted so long, and because she was my mother.

With my mother dying at such a young age, I never got to know her as a friend. Even though she was a teenage mother, she was always my mother.

She told me, "Keia, you will have a lot of friends, but you only get one mother." I was always ashamed of having such young parents. My parents were approximately eight to ten years younger than my friends' parents. Every new friend who met my mother would comment on how young my mother looked. In my mid-twenties I decided that I'm glad my mother had us young because it gave us more years with her before she died.

God always knew that He would call my mother home early. We were the ones who had to come to that understanding and acceptance. My mother wanted to see her children into adulthood. She wanted me to experience dorm life in college, especially since she didn't. I am grateful that God did not call my mother home when she got sick in Germany. He didn't do it when the cancer came back in New Jersey. And He didn't do it when it came back again in Alaska.

Cancer treatment wasn't available in Alaska, so my mother had to fly to Tacoma, Washington, every month. One day, when we were living in Alaska, only my mother and I were at home. I was in my room, and I heard her scream, and then she started crying. I ran into her room and found her in the bathroom. She was holding her hair in her hand. I stared as she kept touching her head and her hair kept coming out in her hand. It was all falling out from the chemotherapy. I was speechless. We just cried together.

My father wanted to go with her to Washington for her treatments, but my brother and I were still in high school, so he couldn't leave us behind. After my brother graduated, my father asked for a transfer to Washington. We moved from Alaska to Washington in the middle of my junior year.

My brother joined the Navy shortly after we moved to Washington. He and my father both were called to fight in Operation Desert Storm. For the first time, my mother and I were living alone. I'll never forget when my mother had to go into the hospital for a week. She stood up in church one Sunday and asked if a family would allow me to stay with them during her hospitalization. I was mortified! She did not discuss this with me beforehand, and I was not afraid to stay at home by myself. I had told her that multiple times. One of the men stood up and said that he had a daughter the same age and that I could stay with them. I don't think I had ever been so angry with my mother. We hadn't been in Washington very long, so I didn't really know the family that I was staying with. I would go visit my mother in the hospital room each day. It wasn't to check on her; it was to let her know that I wasn't talking to her. (I was a seventeen-year-old brat, sorry.) Fortunately, his daughter and I became good friends. She was the one who later introduced me to Jackson State University and told me about Canada.

Hospital Stays

I never had to be my mother's caretaker. My father always took care of everything. He was at her doctor's appointments with her. He tended to her wounds from surgeries. He took care of managing her medication. But when my father left for the war, I became her caretaker as well as her advocate in the hospital.

Although her hospital room changed with each stay, the sounds were always the same. The steady beeping of the heart monitor, almost like a metronome. The occasional hiss of the oxygen tank reminded me of every breath that my mother struggled to take. These sounds, though background noise to some, are thunderous in my memory.

I remember the first time I had to stand up for my mother. During one hospital stay they kept pricking her, taking blood, and giving her new medications. My mother was hurting, crying, and said she was tired. I yelled at one of the nurses when my mother cried out in pain because she pricked my mother in her groin trying to get blood. My father wasn't there to defend her. I was only seventeen years old, but I told the nurse to stop it and leave my mother alone. They would have to try to get blood from another place on another day. I hugged her, and we cried together. We both missed my dad.

I did not know how to be a caretaker at the age of seventeen or eighteen. I regret that I didn't understand the importance of sitting with people who are stuck in a hospital bed all day. Years later, I got a do-over when my little cousin was diagnosed with cancer at the age of fourteen. I visited my cousin often, and I was a good advocate for her. One day she thanked me for being there for her. The day she said that to me, I got in my car and cried my eyes out. It made me realize how much I failed my mother.

Introduction to God

My mother made me read scriptures to her (yes, *made* me). I don't mean every once in a while. I mean every day, multiple times a day. I don't mean one or two verses. I'm talking about chapters of scriptures EVERY SINGLE DAY. Please remember, I was seventeen and eighteen years old. This didn't fall under my idea of fun. Don't remind me that I'm a pastor; I wasn't then.

I realize now that my mother had a two-fold reason for my reading scriptures to her. First, it was comforting for her. I will never forget her being soothed by the words in the Bible. I asked her why she wanted me to keep reading when they were just words. She would smile at me and tell me to read it again.

The second reason I believe my mother asked me to read the scriptures to her insistently is because she knew something that I did not. The Word of God was slowly being grafted into my heart. I was starting to memorize some of the scriptures. I was remembering where some of the books were in the Bible. Who knew that her bratty baby girl would grow to become a pastor and teach others about the Word?

The scripture that I read to her the most was Psalm 91. I would watch her face when I read to her. I remember the first time I saw peace touch the top of her head and transcend down her body. It was as if she were freezing and then someone slowly poured warm water over her. It was amazing to see, but I did not understand what was happening. I was saved, but I did not have a relationship with Jesus. I didn't understand the assurance that the Word of God brings. I didn't know about calling on the Holy Spirit to comfort you. I didn't know God the way that my mother did.

The Last Goodbye

I chose to go to Jackson State University in Jackson, Mississippi (the Sonic Boom of the South). My mother was too sick to fly with me. It's not how I thought I would start college. At the airport, there was a set of twins from high school going to college; they had each other. When I got to JSU, it looked just like the movies. I saw students being dropped off by their parents. Their younger siblings were just as excited to be there. I saw them carrying bags from retail stores. Their parents helped to make beds and decorate their room. I was grateful I had my aunt, Gloria, to help me get settled in.

I didn't know that I would have to get used to not having my mother with me forever. In hindsight, the signs were obvious. My father was called home from the war to be with my mother. A couple of months later, my brother was called home, too. I was in denial about the significance of those events.

My mother was planning to visit me at school during the Thanksgiving break. I was so excited for my parents to see my school. But my dad canceled the trip because my mother was too sick. I called my grandmother and let her know. My grandmother said, "You need to start preparing yourself. Jackie is getting ready to die." I told my grandmother that she was wrong. Mind you, my mother's cancer had gone into remission two times before, so why should this time be any different? My grandmother said, "I watched my husband die from cancer, I'm telling you that I know the signs." How could words that were meant to help hurt so much? The worst part is that deep down, I knew she was right. But I was not ready to say goodbye to my mother. As much as it pained me for my grandmother to tell me to prepare myself for my mother's death, she really helped me more than I can ever say.

Right before Christmas break, a bunch of friends were in our dorm room. Everyone was chatting excitedly about the break. They talked about what they were going to do when they got home, presents to buy, and presents they hoped to receive. They talked about the homecooked food that they had been missing. They talked about going to visit other friends, family, and boyfriends. Everyone was excited about the Christmas break except me. My mother was at home dying.

When I arrived home from college, the first thing that I noticed was that it was hard for my mother to breathe. The cancer had metastasized, and she was in a lot of pain. We used to crush up the pain pills for her so her body could absorb them more quickly. It never helped. I began to pray and ask God to relieve her of her suffering. There was nothing more that this world could do for her. But I knew that God would heal her on the other side. My mother was saved. I was saved. I knew that I would see her again.

I remember the pain and confusion that I felt toward the end of my mother's life. I was confused because she always got better, and I didn't understand why she didn't this time. Our family had been dealing with my mother's cancer off and on for almost a decade. What made this time so different? I was confused because I could not believe that I prayed for God to call my mother home. Confused because as much as my heart hurt that my mother was going to die, I was grateful. I was grateful that she would be able to freely breathe (if that's even needed in heaven). I was grateful that she wasn't going to be pricked anymore. I was glad that she would be free.

One evening my father called a family meeting. For the first time ever, my mother wasn't present; she was in bed. My father asked my brother and me whether we would like the hospital to perform CPR if my mother's heart stopped. My brother said no. I said no. My father said OK. But I wanted to know his answer. He said no. And then I asked what my mother's answer was. He said that she said no, but she would do it if one of us said yes.

My father took my mother to the hospital on the evening of December 25, 1990. I cannot remember what made them go. But I knew that my mother did not want to die at home. She said that she didn't want me to be afraid to live in the house afterwards. I always told her that I wasn't afraid of everything like she was. But she had made her decision, and my father supported her. They did not allow me or my brother to go to the hospital with them.

The morning of December 26, 1990, I walked into my mother's hospital room. She was lying in bed. She was breathing but not with a regular rhythm. I watched her inhale . . . and then finally she would exhale. And then nothing. I watched her chest for any movement. There was none. And then all of a sudden, she would inhale again. Each time it was so long in between the breaths I was positive that each breath would be her last. But then another inhale or exhale would happen. I began counting how many seconds were in between each one. Each time I prayed that it would be her last. I wanted to be with my mother when she died. Although she was in a medically induced coma, I believe she sensed my being there. As I was sitting beside her, I would reach out and touch her hand. But I knew that she did not want to die with me there; she was still trying to shield me from death.

We had been with my mother at the hospital for a couple hours that morning. Each of us spent quality time with her alone. Then we went home for a while. I got my car keys and went to the grocery store. I started with the fruits and vegetables. When I got to the second aisle, I looked up and saw my brother coming towards me. He said, "We have to go to the hospital. Mom died." I left the basket there and followed my brother out. I followed my dad's car to the hospital. We all walked into the hospital together.

The last time I entered my mother's hospital room was the afternoon of December 26, 1990. I never knew that walking into a silent hospital room was worse than one filled with machines beeping. There was no machine monitoring her heart. No oxygen line in her nose. No alarms to alert the hospital staff that something was wrong. Nothing to monitor anymore. My mother was dead.

I took my mother's hand in mine and got down on my knees. My mother's nurse rubbed my back and cried while I prayed. I prayed and thanked God for calling her home. No longer was she in pain. No longer did my father need to hold up her breast, hardened and heavy with cancer, for her to breathe. No longer was her face in anguish with pain. She was finally at peace, finally at rest. *Thank you, God, for healing my mother.*

If you had ever told me that I would pray for my mother to die, I would have called you crazy and told you how wrong you were. But as they say, time brings about a change. The change was not in God, but in me. The goal post never moved; my mother was going to die. I was the one who finally worked my way down the field to the endzone. Or, since my mother loved basketball, I'll say the court and the rim. I was the one who had to come to accept that my mother was going to die.

When I read King Hezekiah's story (Isaiah 38:1–5), I relate it to my mother. God sent Prophet Isaiah to Hezekiah and told him to get his house in order; he was getting ready to die. Hezekiah turned his face to the wall and reminded God of how faithful he had been. God was moved with compassion and sent Isaiah back to Hezekiah to tell him that God was adding fifteen years to his life. The end result did not change—Hezekiah was going to die—but the timing of his death changed because of his faith. I know this doesn't happen for everyone. It definitely didn't with the subsequent deaths in my family.

I wanted to help prepare my mother's body for the funeral. My dad kept telling me that it wasn't allowed. But I was relentless. On his first call to the morgue, the answer was no. But I really wanted to be there, and I begged him to call again. My father called again, and someone finally agreed to let me help with my mother. I was very glad. I wanted to honor my mother one last time. I wanted to comb her hair and learn how to apply her makeup. This was part of my grieving process. We were in Washington, but her body had to be prepared for transfer to Mississippi for burial.

Unfortunately, a huge snowstorm was expected in Washington the day I was supposed to fly out. My father changed my plane ticket and made me leave for Mississippi earlier. I begged him to let me stay so I could go to help my mother, and I could ride in the car with him. But he said no. Driving by himself was part of his grieving process. My brother used a military hop to get to Mississippi. A husband, a son, and a daughter left Washington grieving separately and alone, to bury their wife/mother in Mississippi. I don't recommend it.

We had my mother's funeral and burial in Hollandale, Mississippi. Both of my parents were from the same hometown, so both sides of my family and their friends were there. The churches were too small to hold the funeral, so we had it at Simmons High School. I picked out my mother's casket. It was sky blue with a white dove ascending to heaven. My mother and I were both dressed in white suits with royal blue blouses. My dad and brother wore their military uniforms. My dad's friend in Washington wanted to do something to help, so he bought the headstone. I asked my father to put "Psalm 91" on it.

The funeral was on Saturday. But everything would change on Monday. I had to go back to school. My dad and brother had to return to war. And my mother was left behind in the ground.

My mother used to call me every Saturday morning at 9:00 a.m., my time. That was 7:00 a.m. her time. On normal weekends, 9:00 a.m. was fine. But on those mornings that we didn't make it back to the dorm until 3:00 a.m., it was a little rough because we always stayed up and recapped the night. I always took the call in the phone booth in the hallway for privacy. When I went back to school in January, after the funeral, I really missed her early Saturday morning calls.

I have not been able to write this story without shedding tears. Although the memories still bring me to tears after all these decades, the tears are not debilitating. It was a devastating time in my life. But I have not lived a sad, debilitating life.

I still focus on happy times with our family. I still think of each time we moved to a new state how we'd all go exploring together. I laughed when I moved on my own from Mississippi to West Virginia and I took a phonebook with me. That was a lesson learned from moving around so much (not needed now with the internet). I can still hear my mother's voice saying my name. I still remember my mother's smile.

Back then, I did not understand fully what my mother was doing by having me read scriptures to her over and over. I saw how it benefited her, but I didn't know that it would benefit me one day, too. My mother was showing me that I would not always have her, but I would always have God. He would be with me when she could not. He would comfort me when she could not. I am crying as I write this because I feel my mother's love right now. I see how she was preparing me for life without her but showing me that I never had to live a life without God. Her physical body deteriorated, but her spirit lives on.

WHAT IS CONCRETE?

What is concrete? It is hard.

What is concrete? It is immovable.

What is concrete? Once it is hardened, it cannot be reshaped.

What is concrete? It is what has become of my mother's right breast.

Concrete is heavy on her chest.

Concrete is blocking her breath.

Concrete is crushing her lungs.

Concrete is death.

MY GRANDMOTHER—CLARA MAE JOHNSON, 1995

When my parents married, my mother was seventeen and my father was nineteen, and they had two children. My father joined the Army, and his first duty station was Fort Hood, Texas. It was close enough for us to drive back to Mississippi on long holidays but too far to visit often. We spent nine years in Texas, but after that, we only saw our family every three years in between moves. So, I never had the chance to really get to know my family until I went to college at Jackson State. At times, my grandmother and I were like strangers meeting for the first time. I was eighteen years old staring at the face of a woman whom I resembled. My Uncle Marvin called us the triplets (my grandmother, mother, and me). He said that we looked alike and had the same crooked smile. Hmm, I never noticed that before. (Don't bother looking at my picture; it's not true.) I can't remember who was taller between my grandmother and me. But I'm five foot seven and we both surpassed my mother, who was only five foot three.

I discovered other similarities between my mother and grandmother. They both liked crafts. My grandmother would tell me things about my mother as a child. Since my mother married and moved away so young, she and my grandmother never got to spend a lot of time together as adults. I would tell my mother things about my grandmother. She would laugh about how different my grandmother was then as opposed to when she was a kid. I enjoyed sharing stories with each of them about the other. I became a connection between the two.

One day my grandmother asked me if I liked my name, Keia Katrell. I said yes, and then I asked her why. She told me that she named me, which I knew. Then she said that my mother didn't like her name and changed it. *What? Tell me more.* My mother was born Jacquie Yvette, but she changed her name to Jacqueline Evon. I couldn't wait to call my mother about this. She said that she didn't mind being called Jackie, but she felt like it was a boy's name, and she didn't want it to be her official name. "And your middle name?" I asked. She said she just liked Evon better. After my mother's death, my grandmother and I cleaved together. We kept my mother alive by sharing memories and finding similarities among us all.

My grandmother lived in Glen Allen, Mississippi, about an hour and a half north of Jackson, so I was able to visit often. She had diabetes and I didn't know much about the disease. I remember tasting her sugar-free candy and spitting it out, calling it nasty. She looked down and said, "Well, I can't eat the regular candy." *Ugh, open mouth, insert foot.*

One day my grandmother said that she craved dirt. Yes, I was just as grossed out as you are. What I didn't know then is that it is a sign of severe anemia, an iron deficiency. *Ahh, that's where I got that from.* My grandmother was the first person I had ever seen cooking in a wheelchair. Prosthetic limbs have come a long way since 1990. They were like plastic shells for her to put her legs into with doll-like toes. They tried to match the legs to the color of her skin. She was able to stand in them, but she could not walk very far. But that never stopped her from doing anything. She drove; she fished; she shopped; she lived.

My grandmother didn't lock her door during the day. People came in and out all day calling, "Hey, Clara Mae!" We mostly hung out in her big bedroom, and people knew to come on through. I was still getting to know my extended family and her neighbors and friends. It was so different from how I grew up. Since my father was in the Army, we didn't have any family around. Trust me, the doors were locked.

One morning I was asleep in bed. My phone rang and woke me up. When I answered, I heard, "You have to come home now." I asked why. My uncle, Wayne, said, "Momma just died." I said, "OK," and hung up.

I was numb. She wasn't that sick. How did she die? My fiancé asked what was wrong, and I told him. I called my father. He said that I didn't need to go right away because they would need time to prepare her body and plan the funeral.

I went to work. At the time I worked at Home Quarters in the cash office. I was going through the motions, counting money, calculating totals and recording them. I counted all the ones and put them in bundles of fifty. My coworkers were chatting and laughing. They asked me what was wrong. I said, "Nothing." I kept counting and bundling money. My manager came in and began chatting with everyone. I just kept counting. She asked me what was wrong. I said, "Nothing."

I didn't know how to feel. And I didn't want my grief to spread to them. I didn't even know what my grandmother died from. Why did she die? I was just getting to know her better. We lost my mother, but we had each other. We had so much fun when I visited her. I didn't just love her; I liked her, too. And now she was gone. This was a gut punch that I wasn't expecting. I knew my mother was dying of cancer. I knew that she was going to die, but not my grandmother. I don't even remember the last thing that I said to my grandmother. No one told me that it would be our last conversation, our last call, our last "see you later."

I didn't know how to process that. Why did this happen to me again? I already lost my mother and now five years later, her mother died. What do I do? My dad said to wait before going to Glen Allen. But what do I do when I get there? I just went through the ritual and kept counting the money. I set up the cash trays and placed them in the safe.

My coworkers must have realized that I was not participating in the conversations. This was out of character for me. I didn't even know what they were talking about. Suddenly, they all began asking what was wrong at the same time. All I heard was a chaotic noise that seemed to escalate. I yelled, "Leave me alone! My grandmother just died!" And then I finally cried. But they didn't deserve that. They didn't know. I was so confused and angry. What do you do when your grandmother dies unexpectedly? I felt so robbed . . . again.

I found out that my grandmother had gone to the hospital. She had some health issues and usually stayed a day or two and went back home. That visit should not have been any different, but it was. My grandmother told her sister, my aunt Carolyn, that she was tired; she was not going to leave the hospital. And she didn't.

My great-grandmother said, "I'm not going to live six months behind Clara Mae."

WHERE IS YOUR GRIEF?

When you drive, you look forward, through the windshield. Facing forward, moving forward.

Where is your grief? Is it in the passenger seat right beside you? Can you move it to the back seat, or is it keeping you company up front?

Is your grief in the backseat? Close enough for conversation but not right next to you?

Is your grief in the trunk, out of sight, but still nearby?

Is your grief in the side mirror reminding you that it's closer than it appears?

Is it hiding in your blind spot?

Or is your grief in the rearview window, behind you, but still visible? Where is your grief?

I know what it's like to put grief in the trunk; it's close but hidden from others. And then the moment you slam on your brakes, you hear grief rattling around. Perhaps you forgot grief was there until you got ready to put your luggage or groceries in the trunk. And there grief was, taking up space. So, you move it around instead of taking it out.

When you get home and remove your items from the trunk, what do you do with your grief? Not ready to deal with it yet? So, you close the trunk and save it for another day. When will you decide to unpack your grief and deal with it?

Are you processing your grief, is it moving around or is it stuck? Don't let your grief stay in the car forever.

If you're slowly moving it from the passenger seat to the back seat and then to the trunk, that's progress! Just keep working to remove it from the car.

My grief no longer rides in the car with me. I don't need to fear it; it cannot hurt me. Sometimes a commercial or a comment can cause my grief to appear in the side mirror. I might sit with grief for a moment; I might even shed a tear. But then grief returns to where it was, out of sight, out of mind.

I put my foot on the gas and keep moving forward. Grief is not in my windshield.

Where is your grief? Is it time for your grief to get out of the car?

THE BREAKUP—1995

This is the only chapter that I considered removing from the book. Well, I was past considering. I had decided to eliminate it. I had a friend going through a divorce, and my breakup was nothing compared to what my friend was going through. On top of that, writing this story felt like slicing myself up the middle and exposing my vulnerability to everyone. And let's be honest, who wants to be judged?

What changed my mind? One Saturday after Zumba I told my instructor that I was writing the book. I told her about the different chapters, and I mentioned that I was going to delete "The Breakup" chapter. She asked why. I said because I felt like people would call me stupid for not knowing, or say what others have said, "You were so young; it wasn't that serious." It was serious to me. It was intensely painful to me. Then she said, "That's why you have to include it." Tell people how you got through that grief. She explained that relationship breakups are traumatic, and people respond differently. By the way, she is also a therapist. I got a free session that day. Thanks, Chris!

The Beginning

This relationship started unlike any other that I had ever been in. It was 1990, my freshman year at Jackson State University. He—let's call him "David"—and I were both in the School of Liberal Arts. The first time David approached me, he asked me a question about homework. I asked which one of my classes he was in. He said that we had four classes together. I hadn't noticed. So, I started paying attention. And lo and behold, we really did have four classes together. He expressed interest, but I was already dating someone. We became friends.

I was so excited as I started my junior year, new year, new opportunities. My cousin and I shared an apartment. One day when David was there, my cousin whispered and asked, "Have you looked at David?" *What?* Of course I've looked at him. He'd been there for over an hour. She said, "No, I mean have you really looked at him?" She knew that David liked me. But I didn't share his feelings.

David came out of the restroom, and I looked at him. I mean really looked at him. I hadn't noticed that he had filled out (David used to be very thin). His face had cleared up, and he was looking like a man, not the eighteen-year-old that I met two years earlier. When he turned his back, I looked at my cousin with my eyes wide like, "OMG!" David was fine, and I hadn't even noticed! Later she shook her head and said, "I knew you hadn't really looked at him."

Well, David and I began hanging out more since I wasn't dating anyone at the time. I wasn't ready to start dating again. My previous relationship was with my first love, and I needed a break, but I enjoyed David's company. We had similar life goals, study habits, liked to read the same genre of books, and liked to do some of the same things. We discussed homework, proofread each other's papers, and just overall enjoyed each other's company. We were good friends.

When Valentine's Day rolled around the next year, his friend delivered gifts to me at work. I had a card, a balloon, and candy. I was the envy of the girls at the service desk. The service desk at Home Quarters was in the front of the store and all the customers could see my gifts, too. *Oh, no, I didn't know we were dating! Oh my gosh, how did this happen? When did this happen?* I hadn't bought him anything.

One sentence in the card said, "I hope this isn't too intense for you." It was. I was freaking out. Unfortunately, I didn't get off work until later that night. All the good Valentine's Day stuff was gone. My gifts were lame. I felt so bad, but I had to get him something!

I called him when I got to his dorm. He came downstairs and looked at what I got. He asked if I just bought it, and I admitted that I had. He smiled and said that it was OK. It wasn't.

OK, so now I know we're dating. We had fun. Back in the days of the phone book, they would list free things to do in the city (we were broke college kids). We had the best time exploring Jackson and finding new things to see and do.

I'll never forget the day that David said he picked out wedding rings. I was so shocked. We had talked about our future together, and I knew that we would get married; I just didn't know when. I explained to David that I had observed his family dynamic. Most of the men weren't married; they just lived with women and had children. The two who were married had side chicks. I was not willing to live like any of those women. My mother raised me to be a wife. I also said that he should not put the ring on my finger unless he intended to marry me within one year. I told him, "As much as I love you, I love me more." He agreed.

His friend had driven him around, and he selected a ring at three different stores. He wanted me to pick the one I wanted. The day we went to look at the rings was the day that we had the biggest argument ever (both of us were so nervous). We got to the first place, and I said, "That's the ugliest ring I've ever seen!" The lady at the store was so taken aback that she looked away. We went to the other two stores. Of course, along the way we made up and were back being lovey-dovey. After I had seen all the rings, I admitted that I loved the first ring. So, we went back to the store. The lady was still there; she looked at us hesitantly. I put the ring on again, and I was ecstatic! The lady beamed. It was August 1994, but I couldn't have the ring until Christmas. I used to sneak into the closet and put it on when David wasn't at home.

That year we went to my father's house for Christmas. My dad was stationed in Fort Carson, Colorado. I was anticipating this long soliloquy from David pledging his undying love for me (that's what they do in the romance books). We were both dressed up for this glorious moment. My dad, his wife, and I were all staring at David, waiting. And he got really nervous. He kept fumbling the box, opening and closing his mouth, his Adam's apple bobbed, and he kept licking his lips. He finally said something quickly and gave me the ring. *Whomp, whomp*, let down. But after all the hoopla we took some nice pictures and had a great Christmas together.

If this chapter weren't called "The Breakup," I would tell you all the sweet things David did that made me fall deeply in love with him. They weren't monetary, but thoughtful and sweet. Even to this day, I smile when I think of some of them. But in one brief moment, our whole relationship changed.

One day, I was in the closet, straightening up. David had a duffle bag that he used when visiting between Mississippi and home. I decided to be nice and clean it out. Have you heard the saying, "No good deed goes unpunished"? When I opened the duffle bag, I saw a hot pink card. What is a man doing with a hot pink card? I read it. It was from someone I'll call "Side Chick" (names have been changed to protect the guilty). She lived in his home state. I remembered hearing her name our sophomore year. I remembered him saying that they dated for a few months, but it didn't work out. We were just friends back then, so it was no big deal. I never heard her name again.

I looked at the address on the hot pink envelope. I copied down the return address. A couple of days later I sent her a letter. I wanted to let her know that she was sharing David with me. I didn't want her to be clueless like I was. Side Chick had mailed the card to his friend's house. The card was explicit; it was obvious they were way more than friends. *Oh my gosh, how did I not know? How long had this been going on?*

I felt like the biggest idiot on the planet. Remember the old school cartoons that used to show a sucker over someone's head? That was me: stupid, oblivious, angry, and hurting. I had no idea! I looked down at my engagement ring and cried.

Our apartment was linear. You walked into the living room first, then the kitchen, bathroom, bedroom, and finally the balcony. When David got home, I was in the living room. We greeted each other, and I think he sensed danger. When he got to the kitchen, he couldn't help but see the hot pink card that I propped up on the counter. David never swore but he did that time. *Oh, yeah, baby, it's about to go down!*

What happened next was awful. Well, it was worse than that. It was a lot of fussing, cussing, shouting, screaming, and crying.

I packed up everything of his that I could see. I began throwing things out of the apartment door. I cannot tell you how much I was hurting. I never ever cheated on him. I never even thought about cheating on him. I was never tempted to cheat on him. Everything written in the hot pink card could have been written by me, just swap out our names.

I called my dad. He happened to be home for lunch. I yelled, "Dad, David's cheating on me!" and started crying again. He was shocked! I kept blabbering about what happened. Afterwards my father said, "Well, I'm glad this happened." *Wait a minute! Stop the press! What did you just say?*

He said, "Keia, you've never had your heart broken. If you all had been married for twenty years and this happened, you would have had a nervous breakdown."

"OK, you're right. But this isn't the time to tell me that."

I packed a bag and drove to Hollandale. I remember having to pull off the highway because I was crying so much, I couldn't see. I made it to my aunt Carolyn's house and told her what happened. I spent the night.

When I got back to Jackson, I realized that I didn't want to be at home alone. I drove to Memphis where my brother Alex and his family were. I brought my four-year-old nephew, Ishmael, back to Jackson with me. Taking care of him was the distraction I needed. We played during the day, and I cried at night.

I wanted to call my best friend and cry about my fiancé cheating on me. But what do you do when they are one and the same person?

One day my phone rang. It was Side Chick. I was speechless. She said that she got my letter and decided to call me instead of writing back. Well, once again, the joke was on me. She informed me that she knew all about me. But I needn't worry; she and David weren't in a relationship. They just slept together when he was in town. *Oh, OK, I feel better now. Not!*

She had seen my pictures. She told me all kinds of things about myself and our relationship. She knew that I was getting an engagement ring before I did. It wasn't a hostile conversation. She was relaying information to me. I remember sitting down in the kitchen chair while she talked, astonished. She was so nonchalant about their relationship.

Side Chick also told me how they communicated. He would call her from our apartment and tell her to call him back. His calls were only one minute. His friends and family lived in the same state, so I didn't think anything of it when I saw the phone bill. Then she would call him back, and they'd be chatting while I was either in class or at work. She used his friend's address to send him letters. This is the same friend who delivered my Valentine's Day gifts. And the same friend who drove him around to look for engagement rings. The same friend who delivered her letters to him. Another person who knew what a fool I was. They all had a whole system down that I knew nothing about. Everyone was in on the sham except me.

I was baffled. I told her that I remembered that they dated a few years ago. She said they broke up but never stopped sleeping together. David and I didn't start dating until our junior year. So, did that make *me* the side chick?

I spoke to Side Chick a couple more times. I don't know why I kept torturing myself by listening and asking more questions. But I guess I really wanted to know how big of a fool I really was. She wasn't malicious, just freely sharing information from over the years (with zero remorse I must add). I felt like my heart had been thrown into the shredder and then tossed to the dogs. In case you're wondering why I wasn't yelling at her and cursing her out, it's because she didn't break a vow to me. David did. She didn't cheat on me. David did.

Two weeks later, my father was in Mississippi to move me and my stuff to Colorado. I needed a fresh start. I needed to heal.

My father had remarried and had children. At the time, my younger siblings were between zero and three years old. Every day I would ask the older ones if they had given me a hug that day. They didn't know it, but they were a part of my therapy. I was shattered. I did not have a plan B for my life. David and I were supposed to get married. Grad school was on the horizon. We planned to finish having children by the time we were thirty. At the end of our careers, we were going to foster or adopt children. But all of that was past tense. David cheated on me.

I cried every single day. I was embarrassed. I felt foolish for not knowing. I felt stupid for missing him. I thought that he was my best friend. But what best friend lies during the entire relationship? We started out as friends, not lovers. That should have meant something. But all it told me is that the foundation was never real; it was built on sand.

Was he going to marry me knowing that he was still sleeping with Side Chick?

When I said yes to marrying David, I made a commitment for life. I was all in. My parents got married when my mother was seventeen and my father was nineteen, and they already had my brother and me. It wasn't easy, but by the grace of God, they stayed married until she died. All in. The breakup reignited the grief that I experienced when I lost my mother and then my grandmother. I felt hurt, alone, abandoned, and betrayed.

When David and I broke up, I missed him more as my friend than my lover. But how could he look at me in my face all those years knowing that it was all a lie? Another level of deception. A master manipulator. The relationship that I thought was built on friendship turned out to be based on lies. It was a painful realization. The lies, the deceit, the broken trust, the heartache, the confusion—the breakup. I couldn't stop replaying everything in my head. I was devastated.

Each time I ran into a mutual friend, I wondered if they knew about David's deception. David and I were inseparable, so I had to keep explaining to everyone that we broke up. I was judged by some for being unrealistic. "All men cheat." I do not believe that. "All men are dogs." That's not true. I refuse to give up on authentic, monogamous love because of one incredibly painful breakup.

Little did I know, another death was around the corner.

P.S. If my future husband's name is David, please know that they are not the same person!

WHERE DOES MY LOVE GO?

When you are gone, where does my love go?

The love that was in my eyes when I saw you. Where does it go?

The love that was in my smile when I thought of you. Where does it go?

The love that was on my lips when I kissed you. Where does it go?

The love that was in my arms when I embraced you. Where does it go?

The love that was in my heart because of you. Where does it go?

Where does my love go, when you are no longer here?

Just like that, in one brief moment, everything changed!

I have nowhere to place my love.

What am I supposed to do with my stored-up love?

When you are gone, where does my love go?

MY GREAT-GRANDMOTHER —MYRTLE WOODS, 1996

One of my earliest memories of my great-grandmother was one summer when we went to visit her. We lived in Texas and used to drive to Mississippi. I called her my grandmother, but she was my great-grandmother. My maternal lines are Myrtle, Clara Mae, Jackie, and then me, Keia. When we got to the house, she asked, "What do you want Grandma to make you?" I immediately responded, "Fried green tomatoes and fried okra." To my dismay, she said, "I'm not making that. It's too hot. Now go outside and play." I was crushed. My grandmother's house was the only place that I always got what I wanted.

But I went outside to play like she said to. After a while, she called me into the house. I walked into the kitchen, and guess what I saw? Fried green tomatoes and fried okra! I exclaimed, "Grandma, you made it!" I was so happy! Now many of you probably guessed this was going to happen, but I was little and didn't suspect a thing. Another favorite memory, and yes, it involves food, too, was Mr. Billy's store. It was the neighborhood store, right in the middle of Bee Bee Street (later renamed Martin Luther King Drive). Every day, my grandmother would give me money to buy junk food at Billy's. And every day, I got a honeybun. I mean every single day. (We had to avoid my parents to pull this off.)

As an adult, I realize that my grandmother represented comfort to me. She always gave me hugs and kisses and plenty of good food and called me "Grandma's sweet baby."

After the breakup, I moved from Jackson, Mississippi, to Fort Carson, Colorado (Colorado Springs) with my father. It was beautiful. I was hoping to make a new life there. But eight months later, my father got promoted and was moving to Texas. I couldn't support myself with my job, so I decided to move to Texas with them. He needed time to get housing set up. His wife and kids visited her family in California. I was going to hang out in Mississippi for thirty days and then meet them in Texas.

My dad and I drove from Colorado to Mississippi, it was going to take twenty-two hours. My father was leading the way in his car, and I was following in mine. I had never driven that many hours in one day. My father said not to worry; we would stop and sleep at a gas station for a couple hours. OK, great, because we both had worked that day.

I forgot how long we had been driving, but it was dark, and I was exhausted. I was falling asleep while driving. From time to time, I would hear a horn; that was my father blowing his horn to wake me up. We got to a gas station. I got gas and then I pulled over to the side. I reclined my seat back and prepared to sleep. After a couple of minutes, I heard a knock on my window. It scared me so bad that I jumped! I looked up to see my father with a cup of coffee. I rolled down the window and before I could say anything, he handed me the cup and said, "Let's go."

By the grace of God (and this is not just a saying, I'm serious!), we made it to Hollandale, Mississippi. We both said we were going straight to sleep. It was around 6:00 a.m. and everyone got out of the bed when we arrived. So, we stayed awake, too. It was so nice to see my family again. My brother Alex was there, too.

The joy I felt was short lived. The next day, Easter morning, my great-grandmother died.

That's it. My mother, my grandmother, and my great-grandmother were all gone. At the age of twenty-three, my entire maternal line was gone. That's three people dead in six years. And in between their deaths was the death of a relationship.

In writing this book, I realized that I have blocked some things out. I cannot remember my great-grandmother's funeral. I remember the day that she died. I was driving with my two aunts, Carolyn and Chinetta, following the ambulance. It stopped. The driver and passenger got out. One of them went inside the back of the ambulance. One of them came near us. I went to him and asked if my grandmother was dead. He said that he wasn't allowed to say. I told him that I knew I was crying, but I promised to remain calm if he would just tell me. He didn't say anything. The other EMT was still inside the ambulance; we waited. I asked again to please just tell me whether she was dead or not. He didn't speak, but he looked down. I thanked him. I walked back to my aunts, and we all cried together.

Once they got my grandmother settled into a hospital room, they allowed us to come in and say our goodbyes. I touched my grandmother, and I kissed her. I kept looking at her. I wanted to remember her forever.

I remember being at the gravesite with my dad and my brother. But all the events before that are a blank. Now that I think about it, I don't remember my grandmother Clara Mae's funeral either. I was there when we picked out her casket. It was the same one that we buried my mother in. It was sky blue with a dove ascending to heaven.

WHOLE BUT HOLEY

I am whole.

But grief has taken some holes out of me.

Like a road, my holes have been repaired.

But like the road, I'll never be the same.

I am whole but holey.

My mother's death—a pothole.

My grandmother's death—a sinkhole.

The breakup—a blind hole.

My great-grandmother's death—a wormhole.

My father's death—a blackhole.

Pothole, sinkhole, blind hole, wormhole, blackhole—repaired but not the same.

I was holey after each death, but I am made whole through Jesus Christ.

MY FATHER—TYREE HOLT, JR., 2020

One Monday evening in July 2020, I received a phone call. The caller said that my father had two to twenty-four hours to live. I didn't even know that he was in the hospital. I was devastated. Actually, that's an understatement. I felt blindsided by the news. I was speechless. I was hurt. I was confused as to how he got to that point. Yes, I knew that my father was dealing with some health issues. No, I did not know that he was sick enough to die. He lived in Texas, and I was in Ohio. Now it felt like we were worlds away. My father, my hero. He was in the hospital, and he was going to die.

I called my boss and told him that I was going to work from home the next day because I wasn't sure how I would react when I got "the call."

When I woke up Tuesday morning, I checked my phone. No missed calls. All day Tuesday, I kept checking my phone. I called one of my sisters, and she said that we should go to Texas. I didn't want to be enroute when he died. Wednesday morning, I still had not received the call. I prayed and asked God if He was preserving my father until I got there. I called my sister and asked her if she could get off work Thursday and Friday. She could. I bought a plane ticket and flew to Baton Rouge on Thursday. She drove us to Texas.

We made it to the hospital. Praise God, my father waited for us to get there! This was during COVID-19, so only one person was allowed inside the hospital at a time. The other had to wait outside (not in the lobby, but outside of the hospital, in the Texas July heat). I saw people at the front desk, and that's it. The waiting room was echoey and deserted. It was the weirdest experience.

I was given directions to my father's room. It was creepy walking down long hallways and not seeing another person. I had never been in an empty hospital before. I visited people at nighttime in the hospital; even then there were always others around. But not now. I heard every one of my footsteps on the floor. All the doors were closed, so I didn't hear any machines beeping. The nurse's station was eerily quiet, too. I was so glad when I finally made it to my father's room.

I anointed my father and then prayed for him. I gave him a kiss on his forehead from his sister, Joeann. I sat with him for a while and talked to him. And then I went downstairs and walked back through the empty hallways to go outside so my sister could go in to see our father. I called my brother in the Philippines and told him that I would call him again when I got back to Dad's room so he could speak to our father. Later I held the phone to my father's ear so they could have a private conversation.

I checked to see if my other siblings had spoken to my father. They had. I watched my father struggle to breathe. I thanked him for waiting for me to get there. I told him that it was OK to go. "Dad, I'm going to cry, and I'm going to miss you, but I'll be OK. You're struggling to breathe, and you don't have to stay here for me. I'm going to miss you, but I'll be OK."

I prayed over him one more time. This time I prayed silently. I don't remember everything I said, but something happened to me that has never happened before. As I prayed, sweat poured off me from my forehead, as if someone were pouring water from a cup. I was holding his hand and all of a sudden, he grabbed my hand. I quickly looked at him hoping that his eyes were open. They weren't. But I felt like it was him telling me that he knew I was there. I kissed my dad on the forehead. "Take your rest, Soldier. I'll see you on the other side."

My sister and I went to the hotel. About fifteen minutes later, my baby sister called and said that Dad passed. From Monday evening when I got the initial call to Thursday evening when I got the final call, those were the longest four days of my life. My father was dead, just like that. Less than one week after being notified of his hospitalization, he was gone.

That Friday morning, we checked out of the hotel. My sister and I spent time with one of our cousins and his wife. We were all still in shock at the speed and finality of my father's death. My sister drove me back to the airport in Baton Rouge. I was thankful that God allowed us to see our father before he was called home.

I had to preach that Sunday morning. I didn't have an associate minister to fill in for me. I told everyone to stay at least six feet away because I had been on four planes and around a bunch of people at the airports. I didn't know if I had caught the virus, and I didn't want to risk infecting anyone else. The sweetest reaction I got was from one member who said, "Pastor, I don't care." And she pulled me in for a hug. I really needed that hug.

Because of the COVID-19 restrictions in the US and the Philippines (Alex lived there), we couldn't plan a funeral right away. I took a couple days of bereavement. I made a lot of calls to inform people of Dad's death. I wanted them to know before they saw it on social media. I received calls from some family and my father's friends. I remember my father making calls after my mother died and I closed my door and turned the TV up. It was too much to bear. Now, I was the adult. I was the one who had to make the notification calls. At the end of some calls, I heard, "I'm glad I called. I feel so much better." As a pastor, I was pleased that I could bring them comfort. As the grieving daughter, I was still hurting. Who was going to comfort me?

By that Wednesday, I was mentally and emotionally spent. Once I posted on Facebook about losing my father, I received a lot of condolences and private messages. Then I finally pulled away to work on the Bible study lesson.

A couple hours later, I decided to put a load of clothes in the washer. My washer and dryer are in the basement. I opened the door, turned on the light and gasped. There was water up to the first step. *What in the world was going on?* I went downstairs, but I couldn't figure out where the water was coming from. Everything was soaked! I knew that it rained hard the two days while I was gone, but I never had water issues before. The basement isn't finished, but it contains storage, and I could tell by the waterline on the boxes that it had been even higher.

I took a picture of the equipment and a few other things and texted my neighbor. I asked her if her husband could tell where the water was coming from. She responded and said that he was on his way over. He figured out that my sump pump had quit working. We looked outside, and a drain was clogged, too. I declared that I was going to cry. I was trying to be strong; I had Bible study that night and the message wasn't finished. I just couldn't take anything else. He begged me not to cry. He suggested that I go do what I needed to for Bible study. He would go to eat dinner, and we could look at it afterwards. I agreed not to cry (yet).

After Bible study, I went downstairs, ready to work. Bible study had lifted my spirit. I walked downstairs, and I immediately noticed that all the water was gone. I went outside and the drain was cleared. While I was finishing the Bible study, my neighbor got my sump pump working. And he cleared the drain. I cannot tell you how much this huge act of kindness meant to me. I cried because I don't think he went to eat dinner at all. He worked to clear the water out of my house and from the drain outside. What can I say about my neighbors? They are the best! At a time of major upheaval in my life, it was nice to have someone there. They were the first people I saw when I returned home from Texas. Their words and display of kindness were greatly appreciated.

I went back to work the next day, and that was a huge mistake. I was entitled to five bereavement days, and I should have taken all of them. I was never able to disconnect because I still had to preach on Sunday, host the prayer call on Monday, and teach Bible study on Wednesday. And I was also in school for my Master of Divinity degree, afraid to fall behind. It was all too much! But the only option I had was to keep pushing. I was like a shark; if I stopped swimming, I would drown.

Loving Memories

One of my fondest memories with my father was when we moved to Germany. I remember being asleep and he came into my room to wake me up (I was nine). He told me that it was snowing outside. I didn't believe him, and I rolled over. He rubbed something cold and wet on my cheek and told me that it was snow. I looked at it and said it was just an apple he peeled (ever the skeptic). He finally raised my blinds. I looked outside, jumped up and screamed, "Daddy, it's snowing!" My brother and parents had already been outside having fun before my dad came to wake me up. The snow was cold, fluffy, and beautiful. This is probably what made me fall in love with snow.

When we lived in Fort Dix, New Jersey, my father called a family meeting. He said that we were moving, and he was given the option to pick the next duty station. Our options were New York, Alaska, or Hawaii. We all got our pieces of paper and wrote down our choices. The rules were that the majority wins, and my father was the tie breaker. My dad read off the answers; all four of us picked Alaska. Fort Wainwright, Alaska, here we come!

After my father retired from the Army, he drove trucks for a while. He always visited whenever he came through Jackson, Mississippi. One year for my birthday he brought me a shot glass for every place that we had lived. After that, I started collecting shot glasses for every state and country that I visited and every cruise ship that I went on.

I acknowledged my call to be a preacher in 2009. I knew I was called to preach when I was in my twenties, but who wants to live a consecrated life in their twenties? *Not me!* That April, about six weeks before my thirty-seventh birthday, the calling from God was stronger than ever. But I was scared. I've always done public speaking, so that wasn't the problem. It's that I knew these words carried weight and significance.

One day my father called and the first thing he said was "Are you getting ready to be a pastor?" I was so shocked. I couldn't figure out where this came from. I stammered and told him no. I tried to change the subject. But he asked, "Are you getting ready to be something like that?" Reluctantly, I responded, "Yes." He said OK and changed the subject. "What do you mean, 'OK'? It is not OK!" To understand the importance of this, you must know that my father was not a practicing Christian. This was not a typical conversation for us at all. At the end of the conversation, my father said, "I got to go, Daughter. Acknowledge your calling and move on." *Oh . . . my . . . gosh!* I sat there and prayed, *God, if you used my father, then you really mean it.*

When I prepared for my initial sermon, I was so scared. I called my father the Saturday before and reminded him that I was preaching the next day. He remembered. I asked him if he would pray for me. For the first time in our conversation, there was silence. I got ready to say never mind, but I felt the Lord telling me to remain quiet. He finally said, "OK, but it won't be long." Whew! I told him that with his mustard seed faith I believed that God would hear and answer his prayer. So, each time before I preached, I'd call him and ask him to pray for me. Over time, I got more comfortable preaching. My father called me one Monday evening. He asked when the last time was that I preached. I responded, "Yesterday." He said, "Well, you didn't ask me to pray for you." *Ha, I got him, Mom!*

This was a hard chapter for me to write. Although it's been almost five years since my father passed, I didn't want his chapter to end. Unlike my mother, I did not anticipate my father's passing. My father's death was the termination of my parental care. I was forty-eight when he died, but I still used to ask my father for his advice. He would say, "I know you're not going to listen to me. You're going to pray and do whatever God says." He was right. But I always cared about his opinion. He was my father, but he was also my friend.

SUBTRACTION

The dynamic of our family kept changing, and all I could see was subtraction. We were always a family of four. My brother joined the Navy. Then we were a family of three. My father left for the war. Then we were a family of two. I left for college. My mother was a family of one. Subtraction, subtraction, subtraction.

As my mother's illness progressed, they called my father home from war. A family of two. Then they called my brother home from war. A family of three. I returned home from college. A family of four restored. My mother died. A family of three. My father died. A family of two. Subtraction, subtraction, subtraction.

When I graduated from high school, three were there: my father, my mother, and me.
When I graduated from JSU, three were there: my father, my brother, and me.
When I graduated from MVNU, two were there: my father and me.

When I graduated from RU, one was there: me.

Subtraction, subtraction, subtraction.

Never married, no children. I am a family of one. No addition, just subtraction.

BUT IF NOT

When a loved one is sick, our desire is always for them to get better. The question is, what will we do if they don't? I mean this from a spiritual perspective. How will this affect your relationship with God? If your loved one doesn't get better, will you get mad at God and terminate your relationship with Him? Or will you choose to lean and depend on God for the strength to get through this?

Years ago, I preached at a funeral for a lady from our church. God gave me a message from Daniel 3:8–18. I titled it, "But if Not."

In this passage, Babylon had captured people from Judah. This included three Hebrew boys named Shadrach, Meshach, and Abednego. They had been taught the Torah (the first five books of the Old Testament), and they knew it was forbidden to worship any other god.

King Nebuchadnezzar (from Babylon) made a statue of gold that was ninety feet tall and nine feet wide. Then he gathered all his princes, governors, captains, judges, treasurers, counselors, and sheriffs and all rulers together to dedicate the statue. And the command went forth that whenever the different types of music were played, everyone must bow down and worship the statue or be thrown into the burning fiery furnace.

The three Hebrew boys did not bow down nor worship the statue when the music played. They feared God more than King Nebuchadnezzar or the burning fiery furnace. The boys were reported for not bowing to the statue and brought before the king. The king reminded them of the decree to worship the statue when the music was played. The king added, "But if you refuse, you will be thrown immediately into the blazing furnace. And then what god will be able to rescue you from my power?" (Daniel 3:15).

The three boys responded to the king saying that they will not worship any other gods or worship a golden image. They knew that their God was able to save them from the burning fiery furnace, and out of the king's hand. And they added, "But even if he doesn't, we want to make it clear to you, Your Majesty, that we will never serve your gods or worship the gold statue you have set up" (Daniel 3:18). The King James Version says, "But if not, be it known unto thee, O king, that we will not serve thy gods, nor worship the golden image which thou hast set up."

The boys said they knew that God was able to save them but if God chose not to save them, they still wouldn't worship the golden image. The three Hebrew boys were facing a tragic, painful death if they disobeyed the king's decree. But they chose to obey God's Word about not worshiping any other gods.

So, what does this have to do with losing a loved one? The lady who passed had family, friends and our whole church praying that God would heal her. But she still died. We pray for what we want (healing and recovery), but declare that regardless of the outcome, we will not terminate our relationship with God. God is able to do exceedingly, abundantly above all that I ask or think (Ephesians 3:20), but even if He doesn't, I will still worship Him. But if Not!

When my mother died, I did not get mad at God or walk away from Him. One time my father asked me how I could still love God even though He took my mother from me when I was still young. I admitted that I didn't know. But I did know that my mother had done all that she was supposed to on this earth, and that I would see her again.

When my father died, I was forty-eight years old and a pastor. On his death bed, I prayed to God for my father to wake up and rise from his sick bed. But I also promised God, that even if my dad died that I would still love Him and I would still serve Him and remain faithful.

The choice to heal and deliver is God's. We may not always agree with His decision. And we may not understand His decision. Why does God heal some people and allow others to die? I don't know. Why are some loved ones taken in horrific accidents? I don't know. Why do some people suffer for years only to still die at the end? I don't know.

We must trust that God is fully in control. Some things He actively controls (those things that God commands to be) and some things are passively in His control (the things that He allows to happen). We are usually searching for a definitive answer to "Why?" but we may not ever receive an answer. And we must accept that.

King Nebuchadnezzar was furious with the three Hebrew boys' response. He made his men turn the furnace up seven times hotter than usual. Each boy was bound by their hands and feet, and then he had the three Hebrew boys thrown into the burning fiery furnace. The furnace was so hot that the men who threw them into the furnace were burned up.

The king quickly ran to look inside the furnace. He didn't understand what he was seeing. He verified that only three were thrown into the furnace. But he saw four men walking around! How could they be walking around when they were bound, and where did the fourth person come from? King Nebuchadnezzar described the fourth man as the Son of God.

When the king realized that neither the boys nor their clothing were harmed by the burning fiery furnace, he called for them to be removed. The king realized that their God sent an angel to save their lives and deliver them in honor of their faith. The Hebrew boys did not give up on God or doubt their faith in God just because they were faced with death.

"Then Nebuchadnezzar said, 'Praise to the God of Shadrach, Meshach, and Abednego! He sent his angel to rescue his servants who trusted in him. They defied the king's command and were willing to die rather than serve or worship any god except their own God'" (Daniel 3:28). When we are faithful to God, we are leaving the consequences up to Him. The boys said that God could save them if He wanted to. But even if God chose not to save them, they had no regrets for honoring God and refusing to worship an idol god. But if Not!

Sometimes we overthink situations and try to play God. When you have made your decision ahead of time about what you will and will not do in honor of God's Word, stand on it. Do not waver based on your circumstances. If God chooses to deliver you, He is God. If He chooses not to deliver you, He is still God. As you pray for your loved ones, remember that whether God heals them on earth or in heaven, He is still God! And He is still good! Pray for your heart's desire but accept God's will.

This is a good time for all of us to do a faith checkup. Do you allow circumstances to negatively affect your relationship with God? If so, it's time to make a recommitment and develop that "But if Not" steadfast faith. Vow to still love and serve God, regardless of the outcome.

DEALING WITH GRIEF

Wouldn't it be great if a doctor could write a prescription and tell you exactly what to do to be better in two weeks? Unfortunately, there isn't a time limit or an exact way to deal with grief. But I believe everyone would agree that it is best to deal with grief and move beyond it.

Dealing with grief is kind of like exercise; you must do it for yourself (sorry). I am more faithful when I have a workout partner. So, consider me your partner. Don't give up, we can get through this together. And truthfully, please don't be afraid to reach out for help through a counselor or group therapy. It really does make a difference to speak with people who understand how you're feeling.

In order to move beyond grief, we must deal with it first. There is not a timeline for grief, but "the American Psychological Association (APA) defines grief as lasting from six months to two years. Symptoms gradually improve as time passes."[13]. Although there are some commonalities to dealing with grief, everyone's response to grief is different.

Grief is universal. At some point, it will affect us all. Grief is natural, it is an emotion. Grief is personal. You can have siblings who respond to the loss of a parent differently. There are no rules to grief. You are allowed to feel however you feel. But it's not healthy to remain in a permanent state of grief.

Working Through Grief

My response to each of my parents' deaths was different. They were thirty years apart, but ironically, I was in school for both. I think that being in college when my mother died helped me to deal with my grief. I had a task to complete each day for me to be successful in school—classes to attend, books to read, and papers to write. That's what kept me going for a while. I didn't really share my grief with my roommates or friends because at eighteen, who wants to hear that? I was kind of numb and didn't know how to feel.

I was grateful that my mother was not suffering anymore. But I missed her. I felt like I didn't get a chance to really know her. Even though she was a teenage parent, she was always my mother. She used to say, "You will have a lot of friends, but you only get one mother." She was right. As much as I loved my grandmother, she was not my mother. As years went by and I visited some of her friends, I enjoyed hearing stories about my mother. It was like getting to know her as my friend.

When my father died, I was pastoring Covenant Believers Community Church, working a full-time job, and in school for my Master of Divinity degree. I was functioning on autopilot; I had stuff to do. I worked Monday through Friday. I had to produce a sermon every Sunday, and a Bible study lesson each Wednesday; that required time for study and preparation. We had a prayer call on Mondays, and I had classes for school at night. My weekends were usually for writing papers and finishing sermons. That's what kept me going—I had stuff to do.

A couple of months after my father's death I was confronted by my grief. I was driving to church one Sunday morning. It dawned on me that we would never have our mini-family reunion (my dad, my brother, my nephew, and me) again. It was supposed to happen in May 2020, but COVID-19 was rampant, so we postponed it. My father died in July 2020. *Oh my gosh, my father is dead!* I burst out crying. Thankfully, I was close to the church. I just needed to make it inside.

I cried. I mean I really cried as I finally accepted that my father was dead. I would never talk to him again, ever. *Oh, Lord, please help me!* I sat there rocking and crying and calling on God for help.

My phone rang. It was my aunt Chinetta. Both of us went to church, so it was not typical for her to call me on a Sunday morning. I prayed that everything was OK. I cleared my throat; I didn't want her to know that I was crying. The first thing I heard in her voice was joy! She called to share a praise report with me. I celebrated with her. Afterward, I wasn't crying anymore. But I still needed to be comforted. It was Sunday morning, and I had to preach in two hours, but I was broken.

One of the messages from my Bible study series called *The Names of God* was titled, "Jehovah Shammah," which means "God is there."* I prayed to God and asked Him to comfort me. *God, I need you to minister to me, so I can minister to your people.* Jehovah Shammah, *God, I need you here!* I felt the Holy Spirit wrap His arms around me like a warm blanket. I sat still and reveled in His presence, allowing Him to comfort me. I said a prayer and thanked God for His immediate response. I went to the restroom and washed my face. Then I was ready to minister to others.

While writing this book, I learned that is called a "grief burst." The intense bursts can last for up to thirty minutes. "These bursts are caused by reminders of the deceased person, such as during holidays, the anniversary of the loved one's death, or when giving away items that belonged to the person."[14] Mine was triggered by realizing that we would never have our mini reunion again. It wasn't postponed; it was cancelled.

My father was there for me with all the other deaths and the breakup; now he was gone. Who was going to help me get through his death? I came to the realization that God was there with me through all the deaths and the breakup, too. And God would be the one to help me get through my father's death.

Acceptance does not always come with understanding. We may never understand why a person died when they did. But this is where our faith in God must override our understanding. I cannot explain why some people die young and others get to live to be octogenarians. I cannot explain why my mother was struck with cancer in her early twenties. But I have learned to accept these facts and then find a way to deal with it.

When my parents and grandmothers died, I experienced loss, sadness, and grief. But during the breakup, anger was my primary emotion. When Alannis Morrisette's CD *Jagged Little Pill* came out, I bought it. I resonated with her anger and betrayal. She wrote about her breakup, disappointments, and lessons learned the hard way. I knew the lyrics to all those songs. "Ironic" and "You Ought to Know" were definitely on the repeat list. I photocopied the lyrics to some of the songs, highlighted them, and mailed them to David. Why should I suffer by myself? I was angry and hurt. I felt like I didn't deserve this. After I threw him out of our apartment, he went directly to Side Chick's house. The betrayers were together, and I was alone. Isn't it ironic?

After the breakup, I moved with my father to Colorado. I had a childhood friend who lived about an hour away. When the movie *Waiting to Exhale* was released, I drove up to watch it with her. I cried through the whole movie. The scene with Bernadine Harris (played by Angela Bassett) gathering up her cheating husband's stuff, throwing it outside, and setting it on fire was liberating! She was crying and screaming as she gathered up his stuff. The clean version of what she said was, "Get your stuff, get your stuff and get out!" I was reminded of myself gathering David's stuff, screaming and crying, too. Some of David's stuff went into the luggage and some was thrown outside. I was heartbroken and filled with rage. I bought the VHS when it came out and cried my way through every time I watched it. I also bought the movie soundtrack, but I didn't send any lyrics that time.

I actually felt guilty the first time I went on a date six months later. David and I weren't together anymore. It wasn't like I was cheating on him. But I felt guilty because I never thought I would date anyone else again. I never thought of my life without David. I never imagined myself with any other man. I told the guy what happened and that I probably wouldn't be the best date he ever had. He hung in there with me for about six weeks. I just wasn't ready. Months later I decided that I was going to get past my grief. The song "I Will Survive" by Gloria Gaynor became my new anthem.

Emotional Healing

Have you noticed that when you're grieving, most people struggle to say the right thing? And if you're honest, they never do. It is because there isn't one right thing to say to anyone. The term "I'm sorry for your loss" has become so common that it sounds fake. But I say to give people grace because this phrase gives them something to say. Think about this way: there are many phrases that we say every day, but that doesn't mean that we don't mean them ("Good morning," "I'm sorry," "Happy birthday," "Thank you"). You can determine the person's sincerity.

Even as a Christian, you might not want people to quote scriptures to you. Maybe you want to hear that your loved one is in a better place, or maybe that makes you angry. The stage of grief that you're in may also determine your response to others and their attempts to help.

You can live in a house with other people and still feel alone in your grief. You may all be grieving the same person, and yet you still feel like you're grieving alone. This is because we all respond to grief differently. We go through the stages of grief differently.

I felt alone after the loss of each of my parents. I was staying in the dorm at college trying to process my grief with people I'd just met the previous semester. Each of them still had their mothers. When my father died, I felt alone again. Each of my siblings was spread throughout the country. I did not have any family in Columbus. It was during COVID-19, and I was working from home. I didn't have the opportunity to have lunch with a coworker to discuss my grief. And most importantly, what I really wanted was a hug. I just wanted someone to physically be there with me. If we learned anything during COVID-19 it was how far six feet was—

too far for a hug. Those were difficult times in my life. But I am grateful that it did not become my life.

Choose to actively participate in your emotional healing. Even if you slowly move toward progress, you are moving, and you will get there. But if you remain where you are, you will remain in a state of unrest.

You might have to wrestle with an angel like Jacob did to deal with your grief. In Genesis 32:22–32, Jacob wrestled with the angel all night long. He said, "I will not let go unless you bless me" (v. 26). We must get aggressive and say, "God, I will not let go unless you comfort me. God, I will not let go." My mother and I were both wrestling with her impending death. She came to acceptance of her death sooner than I did. I saw my mother cling to her faith during her illness. I wasn't there yet. I was not ready to accept her death. I just was not ready. But I needed the Lord to get me through the hardest event of my life. I could not do it on my own. *God, I need you to help me!* And He did. He truly did.

Come close to God, and God will come close to you (James 4:8). The truth is that some would never come to Christ if it had not been for the need to be comforted. And that's OK. I joined the church's youth group so I could go to Canada. True story. We lived in Fort Lewis, Washington (near Tacoma). As you know, Washington state borders Canada. My friend mentioned that she was going to Canada. I had never been to Canada. "I want to go!" She said that I had to join the youth group. Done. When the church bus left for Canada, I was on it. See, no shame at all. I didn't join the youth group to get closer to God, but that's what ended up happening.

Why you come to Christ or how you come to Christ is a part of your testimony. The commonality is that we all need Him. No shame there.

None of us can get to heaven without Him. We're all in the same boat. Do not allow shame and pity to prevent you from having a fulfilling relationship with the Lord and His people.

Processing Grief

Having a loved one with a chronic illness can be deceiving. It's easy to think that they've made it all this time, or in my case, all these years, so you assume that they'll pull through this time, too. It's hard to accept that this time it is different. We pray for the person to get better because they always do. *My mother always got better. Why wouldn't she get better this time?* This time was not like the other times. That was the hardest realization to come. This time, she is going to die.

It took a while for that to really sink in. That's why I was so angry at my grandmother when she told me to prepare myself because my mother was going to die. She said it out loud. She said it softly, but I heard it loudly. My mother was going to die! No more surgeries, no more pills, no more tests, no more appointments. My mother was going to die! But I still had to live. I could not terminate my existence. I was still my father's daughter and my brother's sister. I still had a purpose. My mother always wanted me to graduate from college. I had only completed my first semester. I wanted to be a wife and mother, too. I still had to live.

After my mother died, I returned to Jackson State. I studied, hung out with my friends, partied and thought about my mother when I was alone. My father would call from Saudi Arabia when he could. My brother was able to call me sometimes, but we mostly wrote to each other. They both said, "Do good in school, Keia." "OK." I said OK because what else could I do? I didn't have a home to go to; no one was there. I felt so alone. I was so afraid that both would die in the war and leave me completely alone. This was another layer of grief on top of my mother's death.

I was offered an ROTC scholarship, but I turned it down. I was already scared that neither my father nor brother would return from war. I could not make that commitment and then all four of us would be dead. The recruiter called me constantly and begged me to take the scholarship. My father even begged me to take it. My father was enlisted; I would enter as an officer. As an enticement, my father explained that he would have to salute me. I just couldn't do it. A part of me was still scared of my whole family dying. Although I felt completely alone, I didn't want to die. Would I have taken the scholarship if my mother were still living? Probably. Would I have taken the scholarship if my father and brother hadn't gone to war? Probably.

At the end of my freshman year of college, I returned to Fort Lewis, Washington. Fortunately, my father was already home from the war. When I went into my room, I saw a letter and signed blank checks on my bed. It was a note that my father had written after my mother's funeral, before returning to war. He wasn't sure which of us would be back home first. The letter explained how to get the utilities turned on and other things that needed to be done in the house. And the checks were for me to deposit in my bank account. His letter also said goodbye without saying "Goodbye." He didn't know if he would return from war or not.

Later that day I showed the items to my father. He had forgotten about them. He tried to take them both out of my hands. I let him take the checks, but I kept the letter. When my grief was still raw, I used to read my father's letter often. Although it was from him, not my mother, it reminded me that I was loved.

You may find yourself replaying conversations that you had with a loved one and wishing that it had gone differently. Unfortunately, we cannot change that. And it's just bringing guilt and sorrow that cannot be rectified. I have done the same thing. You might feel like you wish you had told them that you loved them one more time. They knew that you loved them.

When I graduated from Regent University with my Master of Divinity, I knew that it could possibly be emotional. It was going to be my first graduation without my father. I graduated from Regent in December 2022, but the ceremony wasn't until May 2023. My friend Carmanita Williamson and my cousin Amaria came to celebrate with me. Everything went great; it wasn't too sad, at least not until Carmanita and I went to the Virginia Beach Boardwalk. They have a Naval Aviation Monument. I began reading the different signs out of curiosity, but that quickly changed. As I read the stories of those who lost loved ones and those who waited for loved ones to come home from the war, it reminded me of my father. As I read and wiped tears from my face, I saw Carmanita slowly walking away to give me some time alone.

I remembered being little when we lived in Texas. Someone knocked on the door. I went with my mother to answer it. A man was standing there. She screamed, hugged, and kissed him. I kicked him in the shin and said, "Stop kissing my mommy!" They both laughed. My mother said, "Keia, it's Tyree." Then my father bent down so I could really see his face. He had grown a beard while he was in the field, and I didn't initially recognize him. Another memory surfaced about my father's time in the field. My brother and I always looked forward to my dad coming home with MREs (meals ready to eat). They were dehydrated meals for the soldiers to eat. My favorites were desserts and fruit.

But there was no denying that the memorial brought back some scary memories, too. When my father and brother were fighting in the war, I never knew if I'd see either of them again. On the rare occasions that I got to speak to my father on the phone, I wanted to hear him say that he loved me. I always asked my father to say, "I love you; I miss you, and goodbye." I wanted those to be the last words that he ever said to me in case he died. He eventually shortened it to, "Love you, miss you, bye!" through gritted teeth. Heaven forbid one of his soldiers overheard him! I cried as I remembered those things. I cried because my father was dead. He planted the seed for me to get my PhD, but he wouldn't be at the graduation. I stood there and grieved the loss of my father. It hurt, but it felt good to let go of the pain that I didn't realize I was carrying.

Afterwards, I found Carmanita and apologized. She said it was OK; she saw that I needed a moment to grieve, and she gave me that space. Then I told her that I realized she was supposed to be at this graduation with me because she was there when my mother died, and she was there as I grieved my father.

I cannot say that the way I have dealt with my grief is either textbook or atypical. What I can say is that by the grace of God, my grief is not active in my life. It was a process that I had to go through after each event. When my grandmother died, it reignited the grief of losing my mother.

I felt cheated because I accepted my mother's death, but I didn't know that my grandmother was going to die. I felt like someone had snatched her away from me. And shortly after that, the big breakup happened. A grief trifecta.

While writing this book over the last couple of months, I have cried a lot; more than in the past years. Writing was like reliving the grief all over again. Memories surfaced that I had forgotten about. At times, I had to get up from my desk and walk away. Grief never goes away. It just slowly diminishes and moves to another section of your life.

One time I was speaking to my nephew Rasheed. I pointed to the entertainment center. I indicated the biggest square and then pointed to the smaller sections. I told him that he had to learn to keep the most important things in the big square and learn to move other things to the smaller sections. I was explaining what it means to compartmentalize. That's the same thing with grief. When grief is new, it's in the biggest square of our lives. It is all that we can focus on. But as we strengthen and move through the stages of grief, it moves from the largest square to a smaller one. And, prayerfully, it keeps moving until it's in the smallest square of our lives. It's not gone; it's still there, but it's not prevalent in our lives.

Finding a group of others who are dealing with grief is a way to lessen the feelings of grief. Listening to others talk about their grief can be therapeutic, too. It lets you know that you are not alone, and your feelings are not irrational. You can also learn healthy coping mechanisms from others.

One of the things that made my mother's death so difficult was all the people expressing their concern. I was eighteen years old, and I became known as "the girl whose mom died," or "Oh, that's the girl whose mom had cancer." Each time someone saw me they would tilt their head to the side and say how sorry they were. The problem was, most of the time that I was out in public it was because I was feeling OK. And then when I ran into people, they brought it back up. I know that they meant well, but sometimes I just needed to get away from being "the girl without a mom." I would just smile and say that I was OK. "'Though people don't often associate them with grief, laughing and smiling are also healthy responses to loss and can be protective,' explains Dr. George Bonanno, who studies how people cope with loss and trauma at Columbia University."[15] I didn't know that this was a defense mechanism. I just wanted to change the subject.

I wish I had known what I'm telling you now. Let people know what you need from them. If you would rather just enjoy the outing (or whatever the event is), say that. If you would like to talk about your loved one, say that. Or if you'd just like someone to sit with you, state that. Learn to use your voice to get through the grieving process. Please understand that no one can read your mind, and it's very easy to misread the signs that you might think are obvious (like my example above).

Each loss changes our identity. I used to say in my sermons, "If I am willing to work on myself, I will be a better pastor, friend, sister, daughter . . ." And I realized for the first time I wasn't someone's daughter anymore. My father was dead. There was no need for me to worry about being a better daughter because I wasn't anyone's daughter anymore. Unfortunately, that realization didn't hit until I was in the middle of preaching. I couldn't stop to process that then. I had to set it to the side to deal with later. Yes, I will always be Jackie and Tyree's daughter, but neither of them was living anymore. My identity changed.

This happens with the loss or change of a spouse. Each time someone sees you, they are looking for your other half. You may not get invited to couples' events anymore because you aren't a couple. You are still the same person, but your identity has changed. It becomes another loss that you're experiencing that you did not have any control over. I read a story about a woman who lost her child. She questioned whether she was still a mother. She felt like her identity had changed. Our feelings while grieving aren't always rational; she's still a mother whether the child she lost was in utero or an adult.

The loss of a loved one can cause one to reevaluate their life. It can cause one to reevaluate their relationship with God. It can cause one to understand that tomorrow is not promised. And some of the things that we thought were so important, we come to realize, aren't. It's time to forgive some people, the living and dead. And definitely forgive yourself.

Assess your life. Look at what you still have, not what you lost. What are some simple changes that you can make to bring joy back into your life? It might be a new habit, a new hobby, or just resuming your old ones.

What we don't want to do is to adopt negative, self-harming behaviors. "These behaviors (drinking to excess, substance use, engaging in risky social or sexual behaviors without thinking of safety) is another way in which people avoid, rather than deal with their grief."[16] I've heard people say that these things brought them relief. Please remember that is temporary—temporary relief with permanent consequences.

You may decide to deal with your grief by journaling. I think that's a healthy way to deal with your grief. I have always written short stories. During my mother's illness in high school and college, the poems were about what death looks like (in colors), and the stories were about happy families (what we were outside of the illness). When I started preaching, my emphasis became the love of God, faith, redemption, and hope through Jesus Christ. So where did this grief book come from? Beats me. But I am grateful that I obeyed the Lord and wrote this book. I didn't realize how much I'd enjoy telling my story, even when it caused me to shed tears. But I truly hope that someone will find help dealing with their grief. I hope that someone will find comfort in the scriptures provided. And if someone strengthens their relationship with Christ, accepts Christ, or returns to Christ, then I know that the angels in heaven will rejoice along with me.

It may not feel like it today, but you will be able to get through your grief. Every day won't feel like it does today. You will smile again when you think of your loved one.

*Bible study lesson from July 29, 2020, "The Names God Jehovah Shammah - The Lord is There," go to https://youtu.be/pNgsXiocRyE.

WHY ME?

I have always said that I lost my maternal-line mothers backwards. My mom died first, then my grandmother then my great-grandmother. Normally, the order is the other way around. I feel like I lost all of them in the wrong order. Why? We'll never know.

That's why the question "Why me?" can never be answered. Why did this happen? Because life happens to us all—the good, the bad, and the ugly. We may never understand the "why" for the losses that we experience.

Solomon, the son of King David, was known as the wisest man who ever lived. He wrote a couple books in the Bible, including the book of Ecclesiastes. The first eight verses of chapter three say that there is a time for everything. Yes, even death: "A time to be born and a time to die. A time to plant and a time to harvest" (Ecclesiastes 3:2). The timing of a person's death is a surprise to us, but never to God.

That verse can trigger anger in some people while they are in their "Why me?" season. You may think, "If God knew that my loved one was going to die, then why did He let it happen?" I don't have an answer for that. Just like I cannot explain why my mother died before her mother and her grandmother. It was her time.

Why did this happen to me? How different would my life have been if I hadn't been introduced to grief so early? If my mother wasn't dying from cancer, would she have rededicated her life to the Lord? If she weren't dying, would she have felt compelled to build a bridge between Jesus and me? Would I have learned to depend on God if I hadn't experienced her death at eighteen? I don't know. What I do know is that all of this has shaped me into who I am. And I don't feel like God owes me an apology for that.

In Job 1, God asked Satan where he had come from. Satan said that he had been patrolling the earth to see what was going on. God asked Satan if he had noticed His servant Job. God then bragged on Job and said that he was the finest man on all the earth. He avoided evil, operated in integrity, and was without blame (Job 1:8). Satan responded and said that was only because God protected him, his home, and his property. And God made him rich, so of course Job lived such a life. But Satan assumed that if God took all of that away, Job would immediately curse God to His face (Job 1:9–11).

God then gave Satan permission to test Job by taking away his possessions, but not his life (Job 1:12). Satan left to do just that. The rest of chapter one tells how Satan killed all of Job's animals, servants, and his children and destroyed his home. Job tore his robe, covered his head in ashes, and fell to the ground to worship. "I came naked from my mother's womb, and I will be naked when I leave. The LORD gave me what I had, and the LORD has taken it away. Praise the name of the LORD!" (Job 1:20). Why me? Why not you?

Job is often recognized for his patience. In him I also see faith, endurance, and perseverance. Through Job I have learned that we cannot control what happens around us or to us, but we can control how we respond to it. We cannot escape the trouble that this world brings. Jesus explained that we would always have trouble in this world (John 16:33). But by being a child a God, we never endure these situations alone. We will never experience grief alone.

Job 42 is the last chapter in the book. God restored Job with double of what he originally had. You may hear some preachers say, "Job got double for his trouble." But the truth is that in all of Job's suffering, he never cursed God or lost his faith. He maintained his integrity. He even prayed for his friends who accused him of sinning. Can God trust you with trouble?

Job's initial response to hearing that his animals, servants, children, and house were destroyed was to praise God. This is what made Job worthy to be presented by God to Satan for testing. As the suffering continued, Job did not lose his faith. He was not happy with his circumstances, which is understandable, but Satan was wrong. Job did not curse God when all his possessions and children were taken away from him. God was right, Job was a man of integrity.

For those who are unlike Job at times and may have expressed anger towards God in response to grief, please know that "The LORD is merciful and compassionate, slow to get angry and filled with unfailing love" (Psalm 145:8). God can handle our emotions; they never deter His love for us. We see God's compassion for humanity from Genesis to Revelation. God sent His Son, Jesus, to pay for the sins of humanity because He knew that humanity would struggle with sin.

During Job's time of testing, he talked to his friends, and he prayed to God (some of the prayers are beautiful poems like Job 14; 28–29). It wasn't easy for Job to be stricken with boils in the midst of his grief. But he endured it all and lived to tell the story.

"We can rejoice, too, when we run into problems and trials, for we know that they help us develop endurance. And endurance develops strength of character, and character strengthens our confident hope of salvation. And this hope will not lead to disappointment. For we know how dearly God loves us, because he has given us the Holy Spirit to fill our hearts with his love" (Romans 5:3–5).

MISERABLE COMFORTERS

This chapter is mainly for those who offer comfort, but also for those who are grieving (I imagine we've all been in both positions before). I'd like to discuss the book of Job again, but from a different perspective.

I taught the book of Job for Bible study one month and every time I read this verse I laugh: "I have heard all this before. What miserable comforters you are!" (Job 16:2).

Remember that Job had lost his children, his livestock, and his servants. And then his body was stricken with boils. Job's friends heard about this and came to comfort him. When they first came to see Job, they were kind to him and concerned about his physical pain and the loss of his family. They sat silently with him for seven days. But Job continued to suffer. The longer the friends stayed, the worse their advice got. They accused Job of sin and told him that he needed to repent. Job told them that he hadn't done anything wrong. They disagreed. His friend Elihu claimed to be speaking on God's behalf. They all determined there was no way all of this would happen to Job unless he had sinned. They kept telling him to repent. And he kept telling them that he had not sinned.

This goes on for many chapters with the friends explaining the necessity for repentance. Finally, Job spoke and said, "What miserable comforters you are!" Instead of comforting Job, the friends ended up accusing him of sin and making him mad. Unfortunately, this is a common occurrence.

Sometimes people claim to be speaking on behalf of God when they try to rationalize events that have happened. "You know, God took (insert loved one) because you did blah blah blah." Really? Did God say that or are those your personal feelings? "You know this wouldn't have happened if you hadn't done blah blah blah." Again, taking your personal thoughts and putting them off on God.

One reason that people turn away from God during times of crisis is because of comments like those. The so-called "comforter" presents God as some vindictive, tit-for-tat God. Sometimes, people get sick and die. That is a fact. Sometimes God heals people and sometimes He doesn't. That is a fact. But that does not determine God's sovereignty or His character. Isaiah 55:8 says, "'My thoughts are nothing like your thoughts,' says the LORD. 'And my ways are far beyond anything you could imagine.'" We cannot, nor should we try to, explain why someone died, beyond the physical facts. The best thing that we can do is show our love and concern for the person who is grieving. Let's not blame God or the grieving person for the loss. Let's not be miserable comforters.

Do not add anything to the Word of God and do not take anything away. Deuteronomy 4:2 NIV says, "Do not add to what I command you and do not subtract from it, but keep the commands of the LORD your God that I give you." Even with good intentions, we cannot speak on behalf of God unless He directs us to. And then, let's use God's words and not our own.

Comforting others can be a difficult task. What is comforting to one person may not be comforting to the next. As the person being comforted, it can be frustrating because no one seems to say the right thing. There isn't one thing or one comment that comforts all people. So, you, as the one being comforted, must extend grace to those who try to offer comfort.

For those who comfort others (which should be all of us, not just pastors), let's be mindful of our words. Job's friends, all four of them, thought they had the authority to speak for God. They accused Job of sin and told him that he needed to repent, then his troubles would go away. Suffering is not always a response to sin. As I said previously, none of us can prevent trouble from ever coming our way. Death, sickness, financial loss, and family troubles can affect us all.

For those who know the story of Job, his friends were wrong. Job was not suffering because of sin (read Job 1). And at the end of the book, God admonished Job's friends, and He defended Job. They were miserable comforters indeed!

The day that my mother died, I called my friend, Carmanita. My dad overheard me and said that he didn't want anyone to come over. He didn't need anyone then, but I did. When she came into my room, she immediately extended her arms to me. We hugged and cried together. That was comforting.

The truth is when you are grieving there are no perfect words to make grief go away. Even as a pastor, I try to offer comfort to those who are grieving, but I know there isn't anything that I can say that will immediately erase that pain. But having someone sit with you is comforting. Having someone call to check on you is comforting. Having someone listen to you whether you're hurting, angry, or confused, is comforting. Receiving cards, letters or emails can be comforting because you can read the words over and over.

Sitting in silence is OK, too. For those who are offering comfort, remember that sometimes just your presence can be comforting. Do not feel obligated to fill the silence with words. Follow the direction of the person you are comforting. Talk if they want to talk or just sit when they just want to sit.

After my father died, my friend Cynthia would call and ask how I was doing. Some days I wanted to talk about it and some days I didn't. She was keen on following my direction and not asking more questions on the days that I didn't want to talk about it. That was helpful because as you know, while grieving, every day is a different day.

And for those who are grieving now, please know that I am praying for you. I promise you that the dark days will lighten. The pain in your heart will ease. You will progress through this grieving season because seasons do change. I wrote this book because I wanted to help others. I had you on my mind and in my heart. Jesus said to the disciples, "Peace I leave with you; my peace I give you. I do not give to you as the world gives. Do not let your hearts be troubled and do not be afraid" (John 14:27 NIV).

DON'T STAY IN THE STATE YOU'RE IN

As I was preparing for a funeral, I thought about all the states that each family member lived in. The deceased was in Illinois, and he had family there. His daughter was in Texas, and he had a sister in Ohio. And then my family came from multiple states, too: Mississippi, Tennessee, Missouri, Ohio, and Texas. The Holy Spirit spoke to me about all those states. The only way his daughter would get from Texas to Illinois was by going through the different states. And in order to go through each state, she had to keep moving.

Mourning is a location, but you cannot stay in that state. Grief is a location, but you cannot stay there. We all must keep moving to get to the next state. As I noted before, there are multiple stages of grief. You may not experience them all, but you will never be able to get beyond your grief without moving. Slow progress is still progress! This is not a competition; this is a fight for your life, your sanity, and your emotional wellbeing.

There are fifty United States, none of them are titled "Grief." So, grief might be your current location, but it cannot be your permanent state. You must keep moving. *Don't stay in the state you're in.*

Please allow yourself to be comforted by others. Remember that it's OK to say what you need—to talk, to sit in silence, help with meals, to find a counselor, etc. And what you need may fluctuate from day to day, and that's OK, too.

Finally, remember that our words have power. Don't ever say that you'll never get over something or that you'll never be able to do such and such again. Proverbs 18:21 says, "The tongue can bring death or life; those who love to talk will reap the consequences." Let's reap positive consequences for our words. *Speak words of life.* *

Philippians 4:6–7 says, "Don't worry about anything; instead, pray about everything. Tell God what you need, and thank him for all he has done. Then you will experience God's peace, which exceeds anything we can understand. His peace will guard our hearts and minds as you live in Christ Jesus." There is a peace that comes from God that truly does pass all worldly understanding. If we continue to focus on being in a state of grief, then we will never move beyond it. Keep your hearts and minds on Christ Jesus. Believe that He will comfort you and bring you through this state of grief. *Don't stay in the state you're in!*

Please repeat after me:

God, I will not remain in a state of grief.
I will keep moving forward.
I trust you, Lord. I trust your decisions. God, you know what is best.
I will continue to honor God with all my heart and soul!
I will not remain in a state of grief!
Amen.

*"Intentionally Speak Words of Faith"
https://www.youtube.com/watch?v=Jv4Q99_s8ow.

LIFE SUPPORT

Let me start by saying that I am not an expert regarding life support. I am not a medical professional either. I was introduced to life support at the end of my mother's life. I know about life support as a pastor and as a family member. I wanted to include this chapter to hopefully give comfort to those who must make a decision for a loved one regarding life support, as well as to offer comfort to those who have already been through the process. Having a loved one on life support can be grueling, especially when you don't know what your loved one's preference would be.

Life support is used when a person's organs are no longer working; the machine does the work for them. "Usually, people use the words life support to refer to a mechanical ventilation machine that helps you breathe even if you're too injured or sick for your lungs to keep working."[17] If your loved one is unable to speak and did not express their desires ahead of time, you may be faced with making a major decision for them. Perhaps this is what you're dealing with now, or maybe you have dealt with this in the past. Anyone who has ever dealt with a loved one on life support has endured a rare and difficult situation. "Remember, your decision is not the cause of your loved one's death. The disease or injury is."[18] If it were possible for your loved one to have a viable life, you wouldn't be dealing with this decision right now.

One way to help with your decision would be to put yourself in their position. This is called "substituted judgment." You imagine what they want for themselves, and then you make the best decision. Some experts believe this is the best way to make a decision.[19] Perhaps your loved one has been diagnosed as brain dead and there is no chance of recovery. Think about what your loved one would want, even if it contradicts what you want. I know it's hard, but please put your loved one first.

My mother chose to sign a DNR. The cancer had metastasized in her body. Her heart was getting weaker. She had reached the point where medicine was not able to manage her pain. Her body was deteriorating. It was a family decision to let my mother pass on her own. The DNR was what was best for my mother. As a family we made the decision to put her above ourselves.

I have sat with families in different stages of this grief. I had one member whose mother was on life support. The doctor said it was time to remove the life support. As you can imagine, this was a very difficult decision for her. I suggested that we go into the little café and pray about it. We prayed together. And then I shared with her what I'm sharing with you: life and death are in God's hands, not ours. As we were talking, the nurse came in to say that her mother had passed. She was spared from making the decision.

But that doesn't happen to everyone. Many are tasked with deciding when to remove the ventilation. If you believe that the decision is really yours, you might feel like you are deciding whether your loved one lives or dies. That would be a heavy burden to bear. But that power is not given to any of us. "The LORD gives both death and life; he brings some down to the grave but raises others up" (1 Samuel 2:6).

Allow me to put my pastor hat on and tell you that the decision for that person to live or die does not depend on those machines, the doctors, or you. Machines do what the body cannot. But God is the giver and receiver of life. Please understand that you may give the direction to disconnect the machines, but you are not making the decision of whether your loved one lives or dies. You cannot control the pumping of their hearts or the inhales and exhales of their lungs. You dictate when the machine stops, but the rest of it is up to God.

When the healthcare worker comes to the family to say that there isn't anything else they can do, they explain what's going on within your loved one's body as well as what will happen when the machines are removed. Don't be afraid to ask questions, you need to be informed and feel comfortable with your decision. If you have any cultural or religious customs, the hospital will honor that, just be sure to communicate with the healthcare team.

When you look at your loved one and you see their chest rising and falling, it seems like they are still alive. And then you tell the doctor to turn off the machine, and their chest no longer rises and falls. You may begin to feel remorse that you "killed" your loved one. But the National Health Institute of the United Kingdom explains that when a person is brain dead, it is the life support machine that causes their heart to beat and lungs to function: "If someone is brain dead, the damage is irreversible and, according to UK law, the person has died."[20] The person is already legally dead; the machines were delaying the inevitable because the person will never regain consciousness and begin breathing on their own again.[21]

For those who may have a loved one who is in the hospital or in hospice and is still mentally functioning, ask the hard question. Have the conversation to find out what that person wants. You want to honor their wish.

This is a difficult situation to be in, and I'm so sorry. We may not all find ourselves in this situation, but some will. You can seek out the hospital's chaplain for comfort. They are not tied to any religion. If you are a person of faith, they will honor that. You are making the best decision for your loved one. You didn't do anything wrong. Please remember that.

Please allow me to pray for you:

Lord, please help your child who is having a hard time right now. Please give your child comfort and guidance on doing what is best for their loved one. And, Father, I pray that you give them your peace through this process and beyond. You, God, are in control. We submit ourselves to your will and your way. In Jesus name I pray, amen.

GOD, YOU ARE NOT ENOUGH!

How many times have you heard someone say that they cannot live without a certain loved one? I cannot count how many people told me that they wouldn't have made it if they lost their mother at eighteen. I used to say that I didn't have a choice but to keep living. As I've aged, though, I realize that I could have handled my grief in a lot of negative ways. But the thought of giving up on life never crossed my mind.

It grieves me to hear people say that they don't want to live without their loved one. They just cannot live without Momma, Daddy, their child, friends, or other family. "(Insert loved one's name) was enough for me to keep living. But you, God, are not enough!" So, was life good enough to keep living for your loved one, but life is not good enough to keep living for the rest of your friends and family? God isn't enough for you to keep living?

When I say this to people, they say that I'm being dramatic and that's not what they mean. But that's the implication of what you're saying when you say that you cannot live without your loved one. What an insult to God, who has never forsaken you. God, who has been there all along. You are telling Him that your loved one was enough for you to keep living, but God the Creator, our Father, is not enough!

Let's change the narrative and ask God to help us continue living a full life without our loved one. Let's ask God for the strength to make it through each day. Ask for help on your sad, angry, frustrating, or depressing days. Instead of getting mad at God, turn to Him for help.

You might feel like God has forsaken you since your loved one died. But trust me, God is still there. If we're honest, we know that people aren't going to live forever. Some people live a long life, while others seemingly die too soon. I cannot explain why or how this happens. But I know that God is still there, in spite of what happened.

Years ago, prior to pastoring, I was in between churches. I had a layover in Chicago. The attendant announced another flight delay. A pastor from Columbus was sitting across from me. He said, "We have to get out of here. People will be looking for us tomorrow." I said, "People will miss you, Pastor. No one will miss me." I was experiencing the grief of not having a church home. I was feeling invisible and unconnected. (I'm not exempt from pity parties either). When I got to work on Monday, I mentioned it to my coworker. She told me all the connections that she saw in my life between work and my personal life. She let me know that I would have been missed.

My first couple of jobs were in fast food, and then I worked in a home improvement store. I didn't know all the regular customers' names, but I remembered their faces and orders. I remembered the houses people were building, gardens they were planting, and projects they were working on. They may not have realized that they had connections, too.

My point is that you matter to someone. Even to people who don't know you by name. And even that is enough to keep living for.

Although you lost a loved one, you are still someone else's loved one. You may be a spouse, parent, grandparent, friend, or coworker. You are still alive, and you still matter to them. Do not make your loved ones who are still living lose you during your period of grief. Go through the stages, deal with the grief, and then decide to move beyond it. Yes, *decide*. It is a choice. Some people don't want to get past their grief. They believe that it defines them. It is a part of your story, a part of your testimony, and it may even become a part of your ministry. But do not allow grief to become your new life. Choose to live, not just be alive!

Please pray with me:

God, thank you for the time that I had with my loved one. Please help me to accept the loss of my loved one. Please help me to have joy in my life again. God, I trust you to take care of me. You are enough for me to choose to live for. I know that better days are ahead. God, you are enough!

PREPARING TO SAY GOODBYE

I understand that everyone is not given an opportunity to say goodbye to their loved one while they are still living. I had the opportunity with both of my parents, but I only took the opportunity with my father.

I did not speak to my mother when she was on her death bed. She was in a medically induced coma. My father, brother, and I all took turns spending time alone with her. I was only eighteen, and I did not know that it was common to speak to your loved one, regardless of their state of consciousness. My mother was the first person I had ever visited in the hospital. She was always conscious and able to hold a conversation. It was not until the last twenty-four hours of her life that she was unconscious. It was weird to see her lying in the bed like that. Although I didn't talk to her, I was there. I sat beside her and touched her hand from time to time. I take comfort in that.

I think I didn't speak to my mother because it felt weird having a one-sided conversation. I wish I had thought to read the Bible to her. Others may take comfort in playing music or reading a book. "Even if the person who is dying is not able to speak, hearing a voice of someone close to them could be comforting."[22]

The last time I saw my father, he was lying in the hospital bed, unconscious. I took his hand in mine. And then I laughed out loud. I said to him, "Gosh, when is the last time I held your hand? It was probably when we were crossing the street. It had to be decades ago." I was forty-eight years old at the time. That memory makes me smile even now. I'd like to think that my father heard me speaking to him and felt me holding his hand. Either way, it's a sweet memory for me. Speak to your loved ones out loud, for them and for you.

The other part of preparing to say goodbye is beginning to release our loved ones prior to their death. "Anticipatory grief occurs before death. It may be felt by the person dying or person's family."[23] It's selfish to ask your dying loved one to hang on for you. I'm sorry if that hurts but hear me out. When you see someone who doesn't have a good quality of life or is in immense pain, it is selfish to ask them to stay here for you. You visit x number of hours a day or week. Perhaps you live in the same home, but you're off to work for eight hours a day. All the while, your loved one lies in the bed all day hurting. Be compassionate and give them permission to leave when they are ready.

If we ask our loved one what they want, the answer may not be the same as ours. Apostle Paul said in Philippians 1:21–23, "For to me, living means living for Christ, and dying is even better. But if I live, I can do more fruitful work for Christ. So I really don't know which is better. I'm torn between two desires: I long to go and be with Christ, which would be far better for me." I imagine our loved ones may feel this way at the end. They want to stay to be here for us, but the spiritual side of them longs to be with the Lord. Unfortunately, they cannot do both.

You must decide what you're going to say to your loved one. Are you going to beg them to fight to stay here or tell them that it's OK to go on? Do you really want them suffering in a body that cannot be repaired on earth, or to return to the Father where there is no pain, suffering, or death? Unfortunately, we cannot have both.

Focus on the quality of life your loved one has. Are they bedridden or dependent on medicine to dull their pain but never able to diminish it? Perhaps they are in a constant state of unconsciousness. What's best for them? Is it time to prepare to say goodbye?

I didn't tell my father or brother that I prayed for God to take my mother. She was in constant pain, she struggled to breathe, and she was hurting in other parts of her body. In my prayer, I told God that I knew He would heal her, just not on earth. And I was going to be OK because I knew that I would see her again.

Everyone cannot handle seeing their friend or loved one in a deteriorating state. You may prefer to remember them as they were. According to palliative care experts from the National Health Service of the UK, "They might find it very upsetting to visit the patient in ICU and they prefer to be updated by family members instead. This is ok."[24] You can choose to send a card to be read by another family member or to leave them a voice message.[25] Remember that dealing with grief does not follow a pattern and it is unique to each individual.

THE FIRST OF FIRSTS

The first Christmas, birthday, anniversary, family reunion, or vacation without your loved one can be hard and very emotional. We immediately think of traditions that will never be the same because our loved ones are gone. The first of firsts. The person who used to carve the turkey might be gone, or the one who used to bake the cakes, or maybe it's the one who used to organize the vacations. And the first event without them may feel empty. These can be challenging times, and it's normal to feel that way.

My mother died on December 26, 1990. My first Christmas without her was different for a couple of reasons. My brother wasn't there; he was still away in the Navy. So, it was just my father and me at home.

My father asked what I wanted for Christmas dinner. I suggested a non-traditional dinner of seafood. He said OK. We went to the grocery store and bought everything. He cooked, and I set the table. We were eating and talking about my mother, making the best of the first Christmas without her.

The phone was ringing constantly throughout the day with friends and family checking on us. During dinner, we let the phone ring. This was during the days of the answering machine. One of my mother's friends screamed in the machine saying how cruel it was to leave my mother's voice on the answering machine. She hung up crying. It wasn't my mother's voice; it was mine.

The call that upset my father was from another caring friend of my mother. She asked what we were eating for dinner, and I proudly rattled off our seafood menu. Lobster, crab legs, shrimp, and side dishes. She said to throw that away and she would bring us real food. My father informed her that he knew how to cook for his daughter. He took the phone off the hook. December 25, 1991, was not a good first Christmas for either of us.

I didn't handle my first graduation without my mother very well. About two or three months before my graduation from Jackson State, the reality that my mother wouldn't be there kicked in. My fiancé finished our last semester doing an internship in his home state, so I was home alone. I began self-sabotaging my grades. I didn't turn in all my assignments; I turned some in late. I was conscious of what I was doing because I still maintained my Dean's List status, but it wasn't my best idea. I knew that none of that would bring my mother back. I knew that it was stupid for me to do that, but I rationalized it by saying that I was only hurting myself. I graduated with honors, but that last semester I had the lowest GPA of my tenure. Grief is not rational. The first of firsts don't always go well.

My suggestion is to create a plan ahead of time of how you would like to handle that day (one day/event at a time). Would you like to spend it with loved ones? Would you like to look at old pictures or home movies? How would you like to deal with your grief on that day?

The other part of dealing with the first of firsts is the reaction we receive from friends and family who are also grieving. They have expectations of how you should deal with these days, too. You must decide whose expectations should be met when they differ. There can even be disagreements between a family unit of parents and children. Have a discussion ahead of time. Let each person express how they feel and how they would like to spend the day. Perhaps there can be compromises around the different celebrations. But please understand, the likelihood that everyone will get what they want is slim. You will have to decide how to handle that. There isn't a right or wrong way to celebrate these days (unless it is something detrimental to your health).

An important thing to remember is that it is OK to be OK. It's OK to laugh and experience joy on that day. It's OK to enjoy your life! That does not diminish the love you have for your loved one. It does not diminish their memory. My father and I loved my mother. But we chose not to spend the whole day crying because we missed her. Although our friends and family were caring and well-meaning, some of their comments made the day worse. But I am grateful that we still chose to celebrate Christmas.

If you have made it through your first of firsts, congratulations. Not everyone makes it, but you did.

NOBODY CARES!

Thinking that nobody cares is a legitimate feeling, but it may not be the reality. When we are hurting, we feel like no one else knows how we feel. It's easy to feel like you're the only person who has ever dealt with death like this. It might sincerely feel that way, but it's not true. That's why there are so many different types of grief counselors, groups, and books to help you deal with grief. The good news is that you are not alone.

When I was writing this book, I discussed and shared different things with friends, family, and associates. I got one of two reactions from all three groups: interest and participation or acknowledgment and a change of subject. Did that second reaction mean that they didn't care? No. I understand that discussing grief can trigger feelings of grief in some people. It causes us to reflect on our own grief, and not everyone is emotionally prepared to handle that. It's not that they don't care, but we all have our limitations.

In Mark 14:32–42, Jesus was in the Garden of Gethsemane. He was preparing for the cross and wanted to pray. He asked His inner circle, Peter, James, and John, to join Him. Jesus told them that His soul was exceedingly sorrowful: "My soul is crushed with grief to the point of death. Stay here and keep watch with me" (v. 34). Jesus went a little further and prayed to the Father. He asked God to remove the cup of suffering from Him (the suffering and wrath that He was about to endure). The answer from God was no. Jesus' response was, "Yet I want your will to be done, not mine" (v. 36).

Jesus returned to Peter, James and John. All three of them were asleep. How could they be asleep at such an important moment for Jesus? Jesus even shared how He was crushed to the point of death. Jesus asked Peter if he was asleep and if he could not pray with Him for one hour. Again, Jesus tells them to keep watch and pray so they wouldn't enter into temptation. "For the spirit is willing, but the body is weak" (v. 38). Jesus returned to praying again. He came back the second time and they were asleep again. Jesus returned to praying to the Father for a third time. And then He found the disciples sleeping *again*! Jesus told them "Go ahead and sleep," but then He was interrupted by His betrayer, Judas.

Did the disciples care about Jesus? Of course. So, why did they go to sleep when Jesus' soul was exceedingly sorrowful, and He asked them to pray with Him? Jesus explained it himself, "For the spirit is willing, but the body is weak." The disciples loved Jesus, and they cared about Him. Unfortunately, although they wanted to help, they were but mere mortals.

Yes, people do care about your grief. But we are all human and limited in our ability to express that love and care sometimes. Even at the most important moments of your life, people will seemingly fail you. But do not give up. Maybe today isn't a good day for them to share in your grief but tomorrow might be better. Maybe that person is still dealing with their own grief and they cannot talk about it yet. Keep searching to find a person or group who can help. And extend a little grace to those who do care but are unable to help right now.

SUICIDE IS NOT THE ANSWER!

If you are not OK, please let someone know. Don't wait for someone to figure it out. Don't wait for everyone to notice that you're having a hard time. It may not be as obvious as you think.

After a person commits suicide, we see the videos of their friends and family saying, "I just saw them," or "I just talked to them." That person did not know that their friend or loved one was struggling and on the edge. Again, the signs may not be obvious.

Please do not suffer in silence. There is help available every day, all day, 24/7/365.

Call or text 988 from anywhere in the United States. You can even chat with them on their website, https://988lifeline.org.

"At the **988 Suicide & Crisis Lifeline**, we understand that life's challenges can sometimes be difficult. Whether you're facing mental health struggles, emotional distress, alcohol or drug use concerns, or just need someone to talk to, our caring counselors are here for you. You are not alone."[26]

Here are some other resources:

- Veterans Crisis Line: Call 988, then press 1 or text 838255
- Substance Abuse and Mental Health Services Administration (SAMHSA): 800-662-4357
- Crisis Text Line: Text HOME to 741-741 in the U.S.[27]

Please read Suicide Help (https://www.helpguide.org/mental-health/suicide-self-harm/are-you-feeling-suicidal), talk to someone you trust, or call a suicide helpline:

- In the U.S., call 1-800-273-8255.
- In the UK, call 08457 90 90 90.
- In Australia, call 13 11 14.
- Or visit IASP (https://findahelpline.com/i/iasp) to find a helpline in your country.[28]

You matter! There is help available for you. Suicide is not the answer!

HOW TO MOVE
BEYOND GRIEF

Grief can be emotionally demanding. It can uncover the insecurity of being alone or the dependencies that we had on our loved ones. And socially it's such a change that it takes time to adjust. "Grieving is the process of working through grief. Providers who help people cope with grief use words like 'working' or 'moving' through grief to highlight the demands grief places on us."[29]

I'll be honest, working or moving through grief is work; however, the benefits will outweigh the effort. You will grow stronger and find yourself being able to process other life events in a different way. "Working through difficult emotions can give you the strength you need to move forward in your life while continuing to hold a place in your heart for the loved ones and life experiences you've lost."[30] The first question you must ask yourself is whether you want to move beyond the grieving period. I understand that not everyone's answer is "Yes." Let's examine that.

Do you feel like you would be dishonoring your loved one if you moved past your grief? You're not. Do you feel like it is a badge of honor to hold on to this grief? It's not. When you live in a state of grief, you are robbing everyone else of yourself and the joy that you bring to their lives. And what about you? You deserve to have a bountiful life, in spite of the loss that you've suffered.

There is not a set length of time for mourning or expressing grief. In the Bible, "The ritual mourning period lasted for a portion of a day (2 Sam 1:12), a single day (2 Sam 3:35), seven days (Gen 50:10; 1 Sam 31:13) or thirty days (Num 20:20; Deut 34:8)."[31] Everyone mourned together. I think I would have enjoyed that because I've usually had to mourn by myself. But to be honest I can't imagine doing it for thirty days straight. That would be emotionally exhausting for me.

So, how long is too long to mourn and grieve? There isn't an answer. Unfortunately, the only way to get through grief is by going through it. What is the proper way to grieve? There aren't any rules for this either. Well, I have one rule, you cannot grieve forever.

My question is, *Do you want to be made whole*? (Again, I don't make any assumptions).

John 5 tells the story about the man at the pool of Bethesda. The pool had five different colored porches, and they were filled with sick people who were blind, lame, or paralyzed. An angel would come to stir up the water and the first person in it would be healed. There was one man who had been lying there for thirty-eight years. Jesus approached him and asked if he wanted to get well (KJV says, "Wilt thou be made whole?"). Jesus asked a simple yes or no question. But the man's response was that each time the water was stirred, someone beat him getting in. Jesus told the man to take up his bedding and walk. The man was able to do it! The man thought the healing was in the pool of water, but the healing was in his faith.

I always wonder, how is it that in thirty-eight years he never managed to wiggle closer to the pool to make sure he'd get in there next time? Even when Jesus asked a yes or no question, the man gave an excuse instead of an answer.

Now I'm asking you: *Do you want to get past your grief?* Yes or no? I believe you do, or you wouldn't be reading this book. So, let's do it! Let's not wallow in pity for thirty-eight years; instead let's begin to thrive. Think about the butterfly. It would never make it to the final stage without going through a metamorphosis. Remember, moving beyond grief doesn't have to be pretty, but it will be productive. *Wilt thou be made whole?*

The first step in moving beyond grief is deciding that you want to.

Guilt can be associated with grief—guilt about being ready to move beyond your grief, guilt about being OK, guilt about being alive and being ready to live your life when your loved one can't. Moving beyond grief does not mean forgetting your loved one. It does not mean that you don't care. Moving beyond grief means not allowing grief to envelop your life. It is an acceptance of the death and your decision to live. Moving beyond grief is finding healthy ways to deal with your grief and accepting that it's OK to be OK. You are not obligated to grieve or mourn for any certain period of time. Do not allow others to make you feel guilty for being OK.

Society tries to place rules on widows. But legally and biblically, the marital obligation ends with the death of the spouse. When or if a man or woman should remarry is their personal decision. Children cannot take the place of a spouse, and living alone is not easy for everyone.

Moving beyond grief doesn't have to be an isolated process. During my times of grief, sometimes I wanted to reminisce by myself and other times I wanted to be around people. The Cleveland Clinic gives five tips for coping with grief. The first tip is, "Practice self-care," including getting enough sleep, eating regularly, and making yourself a priority without guilt.[32] The second tip is, "Stick to a routine" by going to bed and waking at the same time each day to regulate your emotions and establish normalcy.[33] The third tip is, "Attend to your emotions," instead of distracting yourself away from them. They suggest utilizing outward expressions of your grief by crying, journaling, or sharing stories with loved ones.[34] As we all know, burying grief is not healthy, emotionally or physically.

The fourth tip from the Cleveland Clinic is, "Reach out to others," instead of remaining in isolation.[35] Let others know when you need help. It's a reminder that you're not alone and that you still have connections. I talked about this more in the chapter "Suicide Is Not the Answer," but don't wait for other people to notice that you need help. It's not always obvious. And regular people (friends, family, and coworkers) don't always know what to do or say. That's why professionally trained people are a great resource.

Please do not suffer in silence. If you aren't comfortable expressing your grief with a friend or family member, then find an outside, unrelated source. "Men tend to have worse depression and more health problems than women do after the loss. Some researchers think this may be because men tend to have less social support after a loss."[36] The internet can be a great source to find a virtual group if you don't want to meet in person. Or you might want to discover a new group with similar interests. I found a book club and a women's group online.

The last tip is, "Speak to a therapist or grief counselor," because sometimes professional help is needed, especially if your symptoms haven't improved after six months.[37] People deal with grief in different ways. You might do well to join a support group or seek therapy. There are therapists who specialize in grief recovery. It can help to have others who are or have experienced the same situation to talk to. It would be helpful to listen to their healthy coping mechanisms, too.

After the passing of a loved one, it may be challenging to view their belongings (clothes, pictures, or favorite items). Some people find it comforting to keep those items around, whereas others find it too painful. But if seeing their items immediately pulls you back into grief, then you might want to consider placing the items in another part of the house or donating them. This can be difficult when there are multiple people in the household, and each person is grieving differently. There is no right answer. Do whatever works best for you. Create a safe space where everyone can express their feelings and state what they need to deal with their grief and move beyond it.

The goal is to be whole.

Will grief ever go away? Yes and no. Hopefully for everyone the intensity of grief will change over time. I don't grieve for any of my family members anymore. I still love and miss them. But it's rare that I cry about the loss now. When I started writing this book, I was shocked by how many tears I shed. The grief had not gone away. It was tough reaching back to those feelings from the initial loss, but I wanted to be authentic in my writing. My grief is not front and center, but this book proves that it isn't gone forever either.

Why is grief so hard? Because you lost a loved one, a spouse, a friend or a pet, you lost a piece of your heart. It's a loss because a part of your life has been permanently altered. Perhaps that loss affects your identity. And now you're trying to figure out who you are without that person.

Grief can come with hope. We grieve for our loved ones, but we have hope that it won't always hurt this much. We have hope that one day we will smile instead of cry when we think of them. For those of us who are in Christ, we have hope knowing that we will see them again (1 Thessalonians 4:13–14). Though we are grieving today, by faith we know that it will not always be this way.

Grief can be surprising; sometimes, it comes and goes in waves. There were days when I was feeling great, not thinking about anything in particular. And then suddenly, out of nowhere, I missed my loved one. Sometimes I found myself reaching for the phone to call them. Maybe it was triggered by a commercial or a memory, but the grief catches me off guard. I have learned to acknowledge that I miss my loved one. I sit and think about them for a moment, focusing on the good times. Sometimes I shed a tear; sometimes I don't. And then I state that I'm OK. And I continue doing whatever I was doing before.

We will always miss our loved ones. But over time, grief becomes manageable and less prevalent. The tears will turn to smiles.

"To all who mourn in Israel, he will give a crown of beauty for ashes, a joyous blessing instead of mourning, festive praise instead of despair. In their righteousness, they will be like great oaks that the LORD has planted for his own glory" (Isaiah 61:3).

How do you know if you've moved beyond grief? Although we never completely stop grieving, there are signs that we've moved beyond it and are living a life not dominated by grief. For example, there were times that I would write something, and then when I read it, I was shocked. I realized that I had buried that memory, but my subconscious brought it to the forefront as I typed. But I never *remained* in a sad state.

I am able to process death in a different way now. I can see growth in myself from my mother's death in 1990 to my father's death in 2020. Not just because I was thirty years older—I think we all feel like we're too young to lose our parents—but because I had better coping mechanisms.

When my mother died, I was saved but I didn't really have a relationship with God. But I did pray and ask God to help me. The night my mother died I prayed and told God that I didn't want to see my mother anywhere until I got to heaven. I heard about people who felt someone sitting on the bed next to them or that they saw a loved one sitting in a chair. I know that's comforting for some, but it wasn't what I wanted. When I was sad about losing my mother, I thought about the scriptures that she made me read to her. They were comforting to her and that brought comfort to me.

When my father died, I was a pastor who knew how to pray! I had grown in my faith like my mother and found strength in the Word of God. I knew how to encourage myself in the Lord. It's like when my mother died, God held on to me and got me through. But when my father died, I ran to God and held on to Him. I was stronger in the Lord and knew that my strength came from Him. I intentionally sought out the Lord and clung to Him.

I know that I have moved beyond my grief because I do not remain in a grieving or mourning state. Even as I talk with others about my grief or listen to them about theirs, it does not bring down my countenance (a biblical word for face or inner being). I smile when I think of my loved ones. Even when I think about the breakup, it does not bring me down anymore. I have loved and been loved since then. All of these things happened; the events cannot be changed. Yes, they affected me, but they did not destroy me. I am whole, but holey.

So how will you know when you have finally moved beyond your grief? "A final sign that grief is ending occurs when grieving people are able to think about their lost person, place or thing more as a happy past memory and less as a painful present absence."[38] The pain is not as prevalent as it used to be. The sadness doesn't overtake you. And memories can be shared without falling back into a state of grief.

To move beyond grief, assess your comfortability with discussing your loved one with others. Do you want to talk about who you lost? Or would you prefer people not to bring them up? How do you want to move beyond your grief? If you aren't sure, do an assessment during the conversation. If you aren't comfortable, say so.

Some people begin to move beyond grief by clearing out their loved ones' things. As I said earlier, our response to seeing a loved one's pictures and personal items is different. For some it may be triggering and it's better to have it out of sight. Yet for others, it's a reminder of love and happy times. You decide what's best for you.

I truly believe that having someone to talk to is helpful. It may be a friend, pastor, counselor, or support group. It can even be a combination of those things.

A return to life doesn't always indicate moving beyond grief. Moving beyond grief is emotional, not physical; it is an internal process, not external. As long as the desire to heal is there, progress will be made. Remember, even a turtle reaches its destination. Moving beyond grief is a choice. The moment we decide to do so is the beginning of moving beyond it. I didn't like being "the girl whose mom died." I felt like there was so much more to me, and to only be described that way felt so limiting. I didn't want that to be identified that way. Yes, that is a part of my identity, but not the sum of my life.

When you lose a spouse, it's a huge leap to singlehood. Your identity, home life, and activities have all changed. Acceptance doesn't mean that you like the change, just an acknowledgment of that change. To parents who lost babies in utero or on earth, I cannot begin to understand your pain, but I do recognize it. Your identity as a parent hasn't changed, but your family dynamic has.

With the loss of a loved one comes change. Change of the family dynamic, change in your routine, change in you. To move beyond this grief, you must strengthen what remains. After the bereavement period, the emphasis shifts from what was lost to what has remained. Focus on the family that is still here. Focus on the parts of your life that haven't changed. Focus on you. You are still here. You still have purpose. You still have things to do. Strengthen what remains.

Revelation 3:1–6 was a letter written to the church in Sardis. Sardis represented a church that was physically alive but spiritually dead. The warning in verse 2 is, "Wake up! Strengthen what little remains, for even what is left is almost dead. I find that your actions do not meet the requirements of my God." Wake up, get up, break the bondage of your grief, and live! Strengthen what remains: you, your purpose, your family, perhaps your job, but definitely your spirit. Do not allow grief to envelop you and swallow you up. Remember what I said in the first chapter, that like the stages of metamorphosis, dealing with grief isn't pretty. But the emphasis is on surviving to the end, striving for the time to spread your wings and fly. Inhale . . . Exhale . . . Breathe! You are alive! Now live!

HEAVEN

A question that I get asked a lot is, "Is heaven real?" I believe that it is (Revelation 21:1–2). From the Old Testament to the New Testament, God gives us comfort in knowing that we will see our loved ones again in heaven and that it will be a better place.

In the Old Testament, the Bible uses metaphors like "rested with his fathers" (Genesis 47:30; 2 Kings 2:10, 11:21 NKJV) and "gathered to his people" (Genesis 25:8, 17; Genesis 35:29; Genesis 49:33; Numbers 20:26 NKJV) when Abraham, Ishmael, Isaac, Jacob, Moses, and Aaron die. "This 'gathering' is distinct from death and burial (cf. Gen 25:7–8) and implies joining one's ancestors in the afterlife, though the location is never defined and the concept not otherwise developed (though cf. Ps 49:19)."[39] Daniel 12:2–3 says, "Many of those whose bodies lie dead and buried will rise up, some to everlasting life and some to shame and everlasting disgrace. Those who are wise will shine as bright as the sky, and those who lead many to righteousness will shine like the stars forever." In both the Old and New Testament, death was not final for children of God.

In the New Testament, we find comfort in our salvation through Jesus Christ: "I tell you the truth, those who listen to my message and believe in God who sent me have eternal life. They will never be condemned for their sins, but they have already passed from death into life" (John 5:24). Eternal life is granted to all who are in Christ Jesus. "For this is how God loved the world: He gave his one and only Son, so that everyone who believes in him will not perish but have eternal life" (John 3:16). When Jesus was hanging on the cross, He told the repentant thief next to Him, "I assure you, today you will be with me in paradise" (Luke 23:43). We have so much to look forward to.

If you are in Christ—meaning that you are saved—and your loved one was also in Christ, then you will see each other again in heaven. First Thessalonians 4:13–14 promises, "And now, dear brothers and sisters, we want you to know what will happen to the believers who have died so you will not grieve like people who have no hope. For since we believe that Jesus died and was raised to life again, we also believe that when Jesus returns, God will bring back with him the believers who have died." I often say that we are not "like people who have no hope." That's why I know that the death of a loved one is not supposed to make us want to give up on life. We will be reunited again. This is a common scripture quoted during funerals because it is a message of hope.

Jesus told the disciples many times that He would be leaving them to return to the Father. But He did not want them to fear living without Him. Jesus explained that greater things were still yet to come, although He had to leave them: "Don't let your hearts be troubled. Trust in God, and trust also in me. There is more than enough room in my Father's home. If this were not so, would I have told you that I am going to prepare a place for you? When everything is ready, I will come and get you, so that you will always be with me where I am. And you know the way to where I am going" (John 14:1–4). Then Thomas the disciple asked Jesus how they would know the way to follow, and "Jesus told him, 'I am the way, the truth, and the life. No one can come to the Father except through me'" (John 14:6).

I pray that you find joy and laughter in life. I pray that your grieving season does not last long. I pray that your desire to move beyond your grief and embrace the life that lies ahead of you comes soon.

Another question that I get a lot is whether we will know our loved ones in heaven. I believe the answer is yes. In Luke 16:19–31, Jesus tells the parable of the rich man and Lazarus (not the same Lazarus who was raised from the dead). The rich man lived lavishly and dressed in fine linens. Lazarus was a beggar; his body was covered in sores, and he lay at the gate of the rich man every day. He longed to be fed from the rich man's crumbs. One day Lazarus died. The angels carried him to Abraham's side. The rich man also died, and he was buried. While in hell, the rich man looked up and saw Lazarus from afar by Abraham's side. He begged Father Abraham to allow Lazarus to dip his finger in water and cool his tongue because he was in agony.

Jesus used this parable to show us that there is life after this, whether one is in heaven or hell. I believe it also proves that we will recognize one another in heaven. The rich man knew who Lazarus was on earth, but he had never seen Abraham, yet he knew who Abraham was. (I didn't finish telling you the story on purpose. I hope you're intrigued enough to go read it.)

At funerals, we offer words of comfort. For those who are saved, these scriptures are comforting. For those who aren't saved, it can be a reminder that tomorrow is not promised. After death, there are no second chances to get to heaven. Today is a good day for salvation!

The first funeral I officiated was for the family of a newborn baby who did not leave the hospital. My pastor was out of town. He called and asked if I could do it in his place. I had two hours to get dressed, prepare a message, and drive to the hospital. I was so nervous because it was for a newborn, I didn't know any of the family members (they didn't go to our church), and it was my first funeral. I jumped in the shower and started praying for God to give me the right message to comfort the family. The Lord led me to 2 Samuel 12.

King David's son by Bathsheba was sick. David fasted and prayed for his son to get well. He lay on the ground in a sackcloth (a sign of mourning). This went on for seven days. Unfortunately, his son died. David got up, washed, anointed himself, changed his clothes, and worshiped the Lord. Afterwards David went home and had a meal. The staff were amazed. They said that while his son was sick, he fasted and wept, and now that his son has died, David was eating. But David explained to them, "I fasted and wept while the child was alive, for I said, 'Perhaps the LORD will be gracious to me and let the child live'" (2 Samuel 12:22). David had hope that God would heal his son. But now he has a different hope: "Why should I fast when he is dead? Can I bring him back again? I will go to him one day, but he cannot return to me" (2 Samuel 12:23). David understood that his son wasn't coming back, but he believed that one day when he died, he would go to his son.

That last verse was the key to my message to the family who had just lost their baby. We cannot bring the baby back, but, by faith, we know that one day they would be joined again. Separation from our loved ones is temporary. And when we are reunited, it will be for an eternity. There is hope in Christ!

HEAVENLY THINGS

Fellowship with Others

- Matthew 17:3—"Suddenly, Moses and Elijah appeared and began talking with Jesus." The Holy Spirit revealed who Moses and Elijah were to Peter, James and John, although they had never met. Moses and Elijah already knew Jesus. I believe we will know everyone when we get to heaven.

- Matthew 22:30—"For when the dead rise, they will neither marry nor be given in marriage. In this respect they will be like the angels in heaven." This was Jesus' response to the question about a woman who married seven different men and which would be her husband in heaven. All resurrected believers will be in a perfect, glorified relationship with one another. We will know each other, but it will be as brothers and sisters.

A Life of Rest

- Revelation 14:13—"And I heard a voice from heaven saying, 'Write this down: Blessed are those who die in the Lord from now on. Yes, says the Spirit, they are blessed indeed, for they will rest from their hard work; for their good deeds follow them!'" Our good works, or deeds, will follow us. We may not receive recognition on earth for all the good things that we do, but we will receive it in heaven. Then, we will rest from our labor.

Singing

- Revelation 14:2–3—"And I heard a sound from heaven like the roar of mighty ocean waves or the rolling of loud thunder. It was like the sound of many harpists playing together. This great choir sang a wonderful new song in front of the throne of God and before the four living beings and the twenty-four elders. No one could learn this song except the 144,000 who had been redeemed from the earth." There will be musical instruments and singing in heaven. Heaven will have the biggest choir ever!

- Revelation 15:3—"And they were singing the song of Moses, the servant of God, and the song of the Lamb: 'Great and marvelous are your works, O Lord God, the Almighty. Just and true are your ways, O King of the nations.'" The Song of Moses was about the deliverance of God's people from Egypt (Exodus 15:1–18). The Song of the Lamb (John 1:29) is about the deliverance of God's people from Satan's power. Hallelujah!

If you'd like to know more about the day of resurrection, read 1 Corinthians 15. Read Revelation 21 to learn more about what heaven will look like. Also, I did a Bible study lesson titled, "Bible Study – Heavenly Things - A Day in Heaven." You can access it on YouTube here: https://youtube.com/live/6tn45MraeD0.

HOW TO FIND A
CHURCH HOME

If you are like me and you didn't grow up going to church, the phrase "church home" may sound strange. What is a "church home"? It is the church that you decide to join and commit to (your home). There are benefits to having a church home. One is having another family; one that you choose. I shared my story about being stuck in the airport in Chicago on a Saturday, and the pastor said that we needed to get back to Columbus because someone was going to be missing us the next day. Well, I was in between church homes, and no one was going to miss me on Sunday morning. It was a very sad time in my life. I truly experienced grief because I was without a family.

I missed having a church family. I missed seeing the same people each week and catching up with them. I missed having a pastor. I missed serving in ministry. Over the years I had been a church secretary, vacation bible schoolteacher, president of the Missionary Society, over the finance and trustee ministry, as well as participated in all the social events. I missed having that connection. I didn't have any family in Columbus at the time. And the church was the only place that I got hugs.

During this time, I was in a transition state in my walk with Christ. I didn't know that I was going to be called to pastor a church, much less to start one. I was following God's direction in leaving the church that I was in and finding my way to a new location. Each call or text that I received from a friend asking me where I was going on Sunday morning bothered me. My friends didn't understand the grief that I was experiencing. I didn't understand it either. I had never changed church homes while living in the same city. I only left a church because I moved. This was new for me. And for one of the few times in my life, I was a woman without a plan.

My Church Home Experiences

Back in 1989 when we moved to Washington, my mother joined Grace Chapel #9 in Fort Lewis. I was sixteen years old, and I just went to church with her. As an adult in Mississippi, my friend and I were at a night club. She said that she and her daughters were going to church the next day and invited me to join them. I went to church with them and eventually I joined that church. That's where I got baptized! I never had to "find a church home" until I moved to West Virginia in 2005. I moved there for my job; I didn't have any friends or family there. I was thirty-two years old, and I really wanted to keep building my relationship with God. Even though I had been going to church for seven years, I feared that once I moved, I would stop going. So, I really wanted to find some friends in church to keep me grounded.

I started thinking about what I wanted in a church. I knew that I wanted a church where I could make friends. I wanted a church that focused on Bible teaching. I also wanted to go to Sunday school and Bible study.

I had only been to Baptist churches, so I started there. I got the phone book and looked for all the Baptist churches. Well, Huntington, West Virginia, is not very big, so I went to all of them. Then I went to some other denominational churches. After each visit, I made notes about what I liked and didn't like. And then I prayed and asked God to lead me to the right church for me. And He did!

When I moved to Columbus, Ohio, there were more churches to choose from. I made an Excel spreadsheet with the church's name and location, pastor's name, and time of service. Then I had a column for notes. I am not married, nor do I have children, so some activities weren't relevant to me.

But this time, I didn't make it to all the churches on my list. One Christmas morning I was going back to a certain church for the second time. I forgot that Christmas services are usually packed. I couldn't find a good parking spot. I had on stilettos that I didn't want to walk too far in. So, I went back down the street to another church that I had already visited. They had a lot of extra cars, too, but I didn't have a long walk to get into the church.

I had no idea that the Holy Spirit was going to tell me to join. I didn't want to join because this was only my second visit, and I felt like I didn't have enough information to make an informed decision. At the end of the service, the pastor made an altar call, asking people to come down if they would like to join the church, be baptized, or give their life to Christ.

The Lord and I began to have an internal conversation. He was urging me to join. I kept saying no because I didn't have enough information yet. God kept urging me to join. The pastor kept saying that these kinds of decisions take time, and he was willing to wait. *Hmph, he wasn't waiting on me!* I kept refusing to go down there. Well, after a while, I finally yielded to the Holy Spirit, got up, and made my way down the aisle. I went down to the front of the church and told them I'd like to join. The congregation clapped. And then four or five other people came down after me and joined the church, too.

I shared all of that to say that you can have a plan of how you'd like to pick your church home, but if you truly want to be led by Christ, then you will trust Him and join where He directs you. The church may not have all that you desire, but it may still be the right church for you. In your church selection, make sure prayer is always a part of the process. When I prayed about what I wanted and needed in a church home, God placed me exactly where I needed to be. I just didn't know it.

I got what I wanted at each church. I made a lot of friends; it was a Bible-teaching church, and I got involved in Bible study and Sunday school. I eventually became the church secretary (I had been one in Mississippi, too). And wouldn't you know, that's where I acknowledged my calling into the ministry. Although I was very hesitant in joining, God knew exactly where I belonged.

I'm sure some of you may be criticizing me for not obeying the Lord the first time He told me to join. Well, I'm telling my story. And if I said that I always obey the Lord on the first request, I would be lying. Yes, I'm a pastor, but I am also human and I'm being honest. So, be better than me and obey the first time!

When you are selecting a church home, think about what's important to you. Do you want a pastor who explains the scriptures or gives a high-level overview? Do you want a church with families like yours? Are you looking for one that has a daycare, a single's ministry, a widows' group, or young adult groups? If you have no clue, that's not a problem. You can learn a lot from the church website.

If you are nervous about going to church, watching the service online can help you become familiar with the order of service and how they worship. That helps to decrease some of the anxiety. It will also give you some familiarity with the pastor's style of preaching. It can be intimidating going to a new church, especially if you're doing it alone like I was. But I pray that you will find a friendly church home where you can learn, grow stronger in Christ, and make friends.

There are churches that have small groups where you get to know some of the church members on a more intimate level. I love Bible study and Sunday school because you can ask questions in class and sometimes share your story. Having a church home is like having a community. There are usually people at different stages in their relationship with Christ. Some may not have accepted Jesus as their Savior yet, some may have been out of church for years, some may have just walked in a church for the first time. I have been in all three of these stages. And of course, there are the established Christians who are there to help others.

As a pastor, I hope that your emphasis is on the Word (the scriptures from the Bible) that is being preached, but I understand that we all have different desires. And while I have your attention, please allow me to plead on behalf of smaller churches. Please don't ignore the church that doesn't have all the groups or ministries that you're looking for. As the church begins to grow, those things can be added. Focus on what will nourish your spiritual soul. Does the Word that's being preached speak to you? Does it inspire you to learn more and want to live a holy life?

However you select your church home (through your parents, friends, or a spreadsheet), make sure you feel settled in your spirit about it. God will give you a confirmation that you are right where you're supposed to be.

When you are looking for a Bible, find a translation that you can understand. Some common ones are: King James Version (KJV), New International Version (NIV), and New Living Translation (NLT). I preach from the KJV, but I could not understand it when I first started going to church. It has a lot of th's in it: *thee, thou, hither, goeth, doeth, liveth*. But somehow over time, I began to understand it. The NIV and NLT translations are easier to read and understand than KJV. The scripture quotations in this book are from NLT, unless otherwise stated. Look at 1 Corinthians 13 and see which translation you prefer, and then purchase that Bible.

You're welcome to view our services, Covenant Believers Community Church, on Facebook or YouTube on Sundays at 11:00 am ET and Wednesdays at 6:30 p.m. ET. If you're ever in Columbus, Ohio, please stop by and say hello on a Sunday morning. www.covenantbelievers.com

RANDOM REFLECTIONS

I had abdominal surgery, and it really hurt to move. The physical therapist said, "It will never hurt as much as it hurts today." I held on to that. Each time I felt pain, physical or emotional, I repeated that saying. I was acknowledging the pain that I felt that day. And it was a reminder that I would heal.

I thought I had found my soulmate, but he was mating with someone else. I learned that the deficiency was in him, not me.

I don't remember my last conversation with my father. We talked all the time, and it was mostly about absolutely nothing. I had no idea it would be our last conversation. Since I cannot remember it, I focus on the fact that I loved my father, and he loved me.

Grief causes some families to fracture. Grief binds some families together. I pray that yours is the latter.

I began maintaining the birth and death certificates for some of my family members. I guess it is my way to memorialize our family tree. I wanted to do something in lieu of the family pictures that we lost.

Psalm 23:4 KJV: "Yea, though I walk through the valley of the shadow of death, I will fear no evil: for thou art with me; thy rod and thy staff they comfort me." Notice that the text says "through" the valley of the shadow of death. Not parking in it but progressing through it. Everyone walks at different speeds. Just make sure you are walking and not staying in the same place.

Have you ever had a loss that didn't bring you to tears? That's normal. Crying is a way to express emotion, but it is not the only way to express grief.

My mother died at the age of thirty-five. My brother is about two years older than I am. When he turned thirty-five, he said he had morbid feelings, wondering if he would make it to age thirty-six. I, being the smarter younger sister, told him he was crazy. And he was, until I turned thirty-five. And then, out of nowhere, I started wondering if I'd be like my mother and die at a young age. When I turned thirty-six, I thought, "Whew I made it!" (Yes, I called my brother to apologize.)

I have learned that it is a common occurrence. "The death of a loved one can trigger uncertainty and fears about your own mortality, of facing life without that person, or the responsibilities you now face alone."[40]

A disadvantage of being strong or resilient is that people forget that you hurt, too. When my father died, I was often consulted as a pastor by friends and family who loved him. Some forgot that I was also a girl whose daddy died.

It doesn't matter how old someone is when they die, you never want them to die.

Losing someone who had a long-term illness hurts as much as losing someone who was taken quickly. Grief is grief.

DAILY SELF-ASSESSMENT

Be honest with yourself. This is your personal assessment of your current status. I recommend getting a notebook or creating a document on your computer to track your answers and progress. Be sure to add a date each time (you can look back to see how you're progressing). It helps to see your answers in writing. Grief is never resolved in one sitting. We must deal with grief first, and then we can move beyond it.

- ➢ What stage of grief am I in (denial, anger, bargaining, depression, acceptance)?
- ➢ What triggers my grief (places, people, pictures, items)?
- ➢ What can I do to prevent this?
- ➢ What helps to relieve my grief? Is it a healthy coping mechanism? If not, how can I change that?
- ➢ Have I communicated my needs to those who are helping (talking, not talking, just being in their presence)?
- ➢ How do I feel today?
- ➢ Do I feel like I'm moving forward, backward, or not at all?
- ➢ Am I OK with that today?

- ➢ What is/are my goal(s) for today?

- ➢ How is my relationship with God (active, absent, non-existent)?
- ➢ Am I OK with this? If not, what can I do to change it?
- ➢ What can I do today to prepare for tomorrow?
- ➢ Where do I want to be emotionally in thirty days?
- ➢ What about in ninety days?
- ➢ And in six months?
- ➢ How do I imagine my life will be in one year?

Assess your feelings and your progress. Remember that some stages might be skipped, while others may be repeated. All of that is normal.

You are here; you are alive; and now you must thrive!

AFTERWORD

This book has been very therapeutic for me. Memories resurfaced, some good and some painful. New tears were shed. I remembered how much I hurt back then. I remembered the pain of losing each loved one, one by one. But as I shared in "Where Is Your Grief?" my grief does not hurt me anymore. That does not mean that I don't still miss each person that I lost; I do. I regret the events that we will never experience together (conversations, celebrations, etc.), but I do not wish for them to still be here in the last condition that they were in. Each person who died had physical ailments. I would rather them be with the Lord, no longer suffering or in pain, than to be here with me in that condition.

I loved them enough to let them go.

I hope that I have helped someone by sharing my stories. This was not the first book that I was planning to write. But on December 28, 2024, I was listening to a webinar about how to write a book, and God told me to write this one. He gave me the title and major outline just like that!

Writing my story opened another area of vulnerability for me: *What will people say?* I have told parts of my story to friends over the years. I have even shared some of it while preaching or teaching. But I have never shared this much of my life story or my feelings.

As I was writing the book, I discussed different things with family, friends, and strangers. Each conversation was confirmation that this book was needed. But I kept asking if *my* story was needed. Again, the answer was yes. Even in the writing webinars and podcasts that I listened to, writers share the same insecurity of releasing their stories. I am grateful that they told their stories because they helped me, and I hope you feel the same about my telling mine.

Through it all, God has been with me. Although I experienced pain, He shielded me and never allowed the pain to overtake me. I am still standing because He never let go of me. And the same God who did it for me will do it for you. Every butterfly is unique with its own pattern. And so are you; so don't give up.

Be blessed,

Keia

NOTES

[1] "Grief," Dictionary.com, accessed February 26, 2025, https://www.dictionary.com/browse/grief.

[2] Asma Rehman, "How Long Does the Grieving Process Last?" accessed February 26, 2025, https://www.griefrecoveryhouston.com/how-long-does-grieving-process-last/.

[3] "What is grief?" (written September 24, 2024) accessed April 5, 2025, https://hospicefoundation.org/what-is-grief/.

[4] Kimberly Holland, "The Stages of Grief and What to Expect," accessed February 3, 2025, http://healthline.com/health/stages-of-grief#5-stages.

[5] Iris Waichler, "Denial Stage of Grief: Examples, What to Expect, & How to Cope," accessed June 1, 2025, https://www.choosingtherapy.com/denial-stage-of-grief.

[6] Kimberly Holland, "The Stages of Grief and What to Expect," accessed February 3, 2025, http://healthline.com/health/stages-of-grief#5-stages.

[7] Theresa Lupcho, "What is the bargaining stage of grief? How to understand and work through the bargaining process after experiencing loss," accessed June 1, 2025, https://thriveworks.com/help-with/grief-loss/what-is-the-bargaining-stage-of-grief.

[8] Jennifer Fisher, "5 stages of grief: Coping with the loss of a loved one," accessed March 24, 2025, https://www.health.harvard.edu/mind-and-mood/5-stages-of-grief-coping-with-the-loss-of-a-loved-one.

[9] Elisabeth Kübler-Ross, "The Five Stages of Dying," accessed March 24, 2025, https://grief.com/the-five-stages-of-grief/.

[10] Alyssa Jung, "How to Deal With Grief After Suffering a Painful Loss, According to Mental Health Experts," published February 15, 2021, accessed March 27, 2025, https://www.prevention.com/health/mental-health/a35379156/how-to-deal-with-grief/?utm_source=google&utm_medium=cpc&utm_campaign=mgu_ga_pre_md_p mx_hybd_mix_us_20739785489&gad_source=1&gclid=Cj0KCQjwqIm_BhDnARIs

AKBYcmsrzb62wQ0nABA8vmcipU4RAjXlSRSRKqDv11o-
hGMD6hceqHrfi7oaAkxhEALw_wcB.

[11] Alyssa Jung, "How to Deal With Grief After Suffering a Painful Loss, According to Mental Health Experts," published February 15, 2021, accessed March 27, 2025, https://www.prevention.com/health/mental-health/a35379156/how-to-deal-with-grief/?utm_source=google&utm_medium=cpc&utm_campaign=mgu_ga_pre_md_p mx_hybd_mix_us_20739785489&gad_source=1&gclid=Cj0KCQjwqIm_BhDnARIs AKBYcmsrzb62wQ0nABA8vmcipU4RAjXlSRSRKqDv11o-hGMD6hceqHrfi7oaAkxhEALw_wcB.

[12] Melinda Smith, Lawrence Robinson and Jeanne Segal, "Coping with Grief and Loss," accessed March 26, 2025, https://www.helpguide.org/mental-health/grief/coping-with-grief-and-loss.

[13] "Grief," reviewed February 22, 2023, accessed March 27, 2025, https://my.clevelandclinic.org/health/diseases/24787-grief.

[14] "Grief, Bereavement, and Loss (PDQ®)–Patient Version," updated February 12, 2025, accessed March 27, 2025, https://www.cancer.gov/about-cancer/advanced-cancer/caregivers/planning/bereavement-pdq.

[15] "Coping With Grief," accessed March 26, 2025, https://newsinhealth.nih.gov/2017/10/coping-grief.

[16] Asma Rehman, "5 Signs of Incomplete Grief," accessed February 26, 2025, https://www.griefrecoveryhouston.com/4-ways-to-express-grief-that-arent-just-talking-about-it/.

[17] Kathryn Watson, "Making Life Support Decisions," accessed January 23, 2025, https://www.healthline.com/health/making-life-support-decisions.

[18] "Removing Life Support," accessed January 23, 2025, https://www.saintlukeskc.org/health-library/removing-life-support.

[19] "Making Decisions for Someone at the End of Life," accessed March 27, 2025, https://www.nia.nih.gov/health/end-life/making-decisions-someone-end-life.

[20] "Overview—Brain Death," Reviewed September 8, 2022, accessed January 24, 2025, https://www.nhs.uk/conditions/brain-death/.

[21] "Overview—Brain Death," Reviewed September 8, 2022, accessed January 24, 2025, https://www.nhs.uk/conditions/brain-death/.

[22] Catherine White, Dr. Kathryn Manni, Professor Natalie Pattison, and Dr. Joe Cosgrove, "End of life in intensive care," accessed March 30, 2025, https://icusteps.org/information/information-sheets/end-of-life.

[23] Updated February 12, 2025, "Grief, Bereavement, and Loss (PDQ®)–Patient Version," accessed March 27, 2025, https://www.cancer.gov/about-cancer/advanced-cancer/caregivers/planning/bereavement-pdq.

[24] Catherine White, "End of life in intensive care," accessed March 30, 2025, https://icusteps.org/information/information-sheets/end-of-life.

[25] Catherine White, "End of life in intensive care," accessed March 30, 2025, https://icusteps.org/information/information-sheets/end-of-life.

[26] Accessed March 16, 2025, https://988lifeline.org/.

[27] Jennifer Fisher, "5 stages of grief: Coping with the loss of a loved one," accessed March 24, 2025, https://www.health.harvard.edu/mind-and-mood/5-stages-of-grief-coping-with-the-loss-of-a-loved-one.

[28] Melinda Smith, Lawrence Robinson, Jeanne Segal, "Coping with Grief and Loss," accessed March 26, 2025, https://www.helpguide.org/mental-health/grief/coping-with-grief-and-loss.

[29] "Grief," last reviewed February 22, 2023, https://my.clevelandclinic.org/health/diseases/24787-grief.

[30] "Grief," last reviewed February 22, 2023, https://my.clevelandclinic.org/health/diseases/24787-grief.

[31] M. J. Boda, "1. Lament and Mourning in the Prophets as Oral Artifact," in *Dictionary of Old Testament Prophets*, ed. Mark J. Boda, J. Gordon McConville (Downers Grove: InterVarsity Press, 2012), 473.

[32] "Grief," last reviewed February 22, 2023, accessed March 27, 2025, https://my.clevelandclinic.org/health/diseases/24787-grief.

[33] "Grief," last reviewed February 22, 2023, accessed March 27, 2025, https://my.clevelandclinic.org/health/diseases/24787-grief.

[34] "Grief," last reviewed February 22, 2023, accessed March 27, 2025, https://my.clevelandclinic.org/health/diseases/24787-grief.

[35] "Grief," last reviewed February 22, 2023, accessed March 27, 2025, https://my.clevelandclinic.org/health/diseases/24787-grief.

[36] "Grief, Bereavement, and Loss (PDQ)–Patient Version," accessed March 27, 2025, https://www.cancer.gov/about-cancer/advanced-cancer/caregivers/planning/bereavement-pdq.

[37] "Grief," last reviewed February 22, 2023, accessed March 27, 2025, https://my.clevelandclinic.org/health/diseases/24787-grief.

[38] "Understanding When Grief Is Complete," accessed February 24, 2025, https://www.mentalhealth.com/library/understanding-when-grief-is-complete#:~:text=A%20final%20sign%20that%20grief,acute%20as%20it%20once%20was.

[39] P. S. Johnston, "3.3. Death and the Dead," in *Dictionary of the Old Testament Pentateuch*, ed. David Baker, T. Desmond Alexander (Downers Grove: InterVarsity Press, 2003), 536.

[40] Melinda Smith, "Coping with Grief and Loss," accessed 3/26/2025, https://www.helpguide.org/mental-health/grief/coping-with-grief-and-loss.

www.ingramcontent.com/pod-product-compliance
Lightning Source LLC
Chambersburg PA
CBHW071307130626
46556CB00004B/1497